Work *After* Baby

Work *After* Baby

The Christian Mum's Guide to Work *After* Maternity Leave

MARYKE JESUDASON

RESOURCE *Publications* • Eugene, Oregon

WORK AFTER BABY
The Christian Mum's Guide to Work After Maternity Leave

Resource Publications
An Imprint of Wipf and Stock Publishers
199 W. 8th Ave., Suite 3
Eugene, OR 97401

www.wipfandstock.com

PAPERBACK ISBN: 979-8-3852-4163-7
HARDCOVER ISBN: 979-8-3852-4164-4
EBOOK ISBN: 979-8-3852-4165-1

04/23/25

To my wonderful husband, who supports me and loves me more than I deserve. To my beautiful boy, who brightens every day just by being there. And to the little one on the way, I can't wait to meet you.

Contents

CONTENTS

Acknowledgments

A SPECIAL THANK YOU to the fellow mothers in Christ who shared their valuable insights, reflections and advice via the survey so that other mums can be supported through this book.

Thank you to Vicine Koroma, Jana Berker and an anonymous friend who agreed to be interviewed for this book. As career development professionals and ministry workers, your guidance has been invaluable. Thank you for your wisdom and love for Jesus.

Introduction

WELL, HELLO YOU LOVELY mum. So, you're going back to work? Me too. At least we're in this together. Let me introduce myself.

I am a slacker. I love nothing more than to sit back and take the easy option. Laziness and I are the best of friends, and we certainly do not part ways when it comes to work*. In fact, it's where we thrive.

A few years back in my career, I didn't get the promotion I felt I was entitled to. I felt angry and defeated. I worked so hard and for what? So, I decided 'screw it, why bother putting in more effort when I can just do the bare minimum and still get the salary'. I knew it was wrong, that it wasn't very "Christian" of me, but I avoided thinking about it too much because I knew I'd be convicted and have to change my ways. I liked the comfortable cruise I was on.

Fast forward to the last few months of maternity leave, through unrelated chats with Christian friends, I saw their integrity towards their work. The way they talked about their jobs was filled with love for others and for God. Then the Holy Spirit did that nudgey thing where He prompts you to seriously reflect and repent. I'd never spent much time meditating on what God says about work. I realised that I would soon be going back to my paid job, and this was an opportunity to learn how to be a Christian in the workplace. So that's what I did. I read and prayed and talked to mentors and friends and listened to sermons. I was deeply challenged by what I discovered and saw my foolishness in waiting this long to learn something so good.

I'm so thankful that God uses this clear point in time, unique to many Christian mothers - the return to employment after mat leave. And that return comes with so many complexities regarding faith, practicalities, emotions and relationships.

This book is going to unpack all of that, using advice and experience from real Jesus-loving mums to tell you how they managed going back to work. We'll look at the impact on faith and what God says about work, the practical considerations, how the relationships with your husband, child, colleagues and friends may be impacted, and your emotional side too.

Let's get to work, ladies.

*I am using the term 'work' in this book to describe paid employment but of course our role as mothers is very much work and very much a full time job.

The Bible Stuff

The Bible Stuff

Natural Connections

WHEN I THINK OF ministry, I naturally fall into the trap of thinking of overseas mission, helping out at a homeless shelter or street evangelism (all good things of course). I thought that it meant going out of your way to jump into an unfamiliar environment and do something uncomfortable, to try and get people to love Jesus or invite them along to Church.

If only there was somewhere where many Christians are naturally rubbing shoulders with non-Christians. . . oh, wait. How many of us have jobs in the secular environment? Answer—most of us! The majority of us are not in paid Church ministry roles, nor should we be. That is a calling for a select few. Some of us are called to work in a cafe making drinks, an office writing reports, a van delivering food and so on. All are good. The wonderful thing about my office job is that I am for 3 days a week (I'm a part-timer), naturally connecting with a dozen non-Christians. That's hundreds of hours each year these non-believers are with someone who knows Jesus. God knows and loves me, and He knows and loves my colleagues, and He has chosen little old me to be in their lives. There is purpose to our lives intertwining. What an honour.

The God Who Works

Our transition back to work is a great opportunity to learn what God says about work. Am I about to do that classic Christian book thing where I say we have to start at Genesis to truly grasp the topic at hand? Yes, yes I am. But His word is clear, it doesn't need my waffle, so I'll keep it brief. I think there are three big things Genesis teaches us about work:

1. God worked to create the world in six days and then he rested. What he made was good.

"By the seventh day God had finished the work he had been doing; so on the seventh day he rested from all his work. Then God blessed the seventh day and made it holy, because on it he rested from all the work of creating that he had done." (Genesis 2:2–3)

2. God designed us to reflect His image and part of His image is to work.

"Then God said, "Let us make mankind in our image, in our likeness, so that they may rule over the fish in the sea and the birds in the sky, over the livestock and all the wild animals, and over all the creatures that move along the ground." (Genesis 1:26)

3. Work is good but the fall made work difficult.

"To Adam he said, "Because you listened to your wife and ate fruit from the tree about which I commanded you, 'You must not eat from it,' "Cursed is the ground because of you: through painful toil you will eat food from it all the days of your life. It will produce thorns and thistles for you, and you will eat the plants of the field. By the sweat of your brow you will eat your food until you return to the ground, since from it you were taken; for dust you are and to dust you will return." (Genesis 3:17–19)

Jesus and Work

Jesus had a secular job as a carpenter, while working to bring people to the Father through Him. His attitude towards work was built on glorifying His Heavenly Father.

"I have brought you glory on earth by finishing the work you gave me to do." (John 17:4)

We are created in Christ Jesus for good works. His death on the cross means salvation for those who believe. God has placed us to showcase this grace in our workplaces and glorify Him. Our salvation in Jesus means our work has a purpose. This purpose is and always will be to glorify God. No matter what job you do, its core purpose will never ever change.

"For by grace you have been saved through faith. And this is not your own doing; it is the gift of God, not a result of works, so that no one may boast. For we are his workmanship, created in Christ Jesus for good works, which God prepared beforehand, that we should walk in them." (Ephesians 2:8–10)

"So whether you eat or drink or whatever you do, do it all for the glory of God." (1 Corinthians 10:31)

Biblical Examples of Working Women: Ancient Wisdom for Modern Mums

As modern working mothers, we often grapple with questions about balancing career and family life. Yet, the Bible provides us with rich examples of women who successfully navigated multiple roles, showing us that this isn't a modern dilemma but rather a timeless journey of faithful service. "Whatever you do, work at it with all your heart, as working for the Lord, not for human masters" (Colossians 3:23).

Perhaps the most well-known example is the Proverbs 31 woman, whose life reads remarkably like a modern working mother's CV. "She considers a field and buys it; out of her earnings she plants a vineyard. . . She sees that her trading is profitable, and her lamp does not go out at night" (Proverbs 31:16,18). She's a skilled businesswoman dealing in textiles and real estate, manages household staff, and oversees complex operations while ensuring her family thrives. "She watches over the affairs of her household and does not eat the bread of idleness" (Proverbs 31:27). Far from presenting this as problematic, Scripture holds her up as an example of godly womanhood. Her example reassures us that commercial activity and family care aren't mutually exclusive but can be woven together in a life that honours God.

Also consider Deborah, who balanced roles as a prophet, judge, and military strategist. "Now Deborah, a prophet, the wife of Lappidoth, was leading Israel at that time. She held court under the Palm of Deborah. . . and the Israelites went up to her to have their disputes decided" (Judges 4:4–5). Her leadership wasn't presented as being in tension with family life but as a natural expression of her God-given gifts. As women, we can be leaders in the workplace. Deborah was confident that God goes before us (Judges 4:14) and we can be too.

Ruth's story speaks particularly to those of us who work out of necessity. "So, Ruth gleaned in the field until evening. Then she threshed the barley she had gathered, and it amounted to about an ephah" (Ruth 2:17). As a widow working in the fields to provide for her family, she demonstrated that hard work with the right motives honours God. Her dedication to providing for her family through honest labour reflects the reality of many working mothers today.

Tabitha (also known as Dorcas) used her skills as a seamstress to impact her community significantly. "In Joppa there was a disciple named Tabitha. . . who was always doing good and helping the poor. She became sick and died, and. . . all the widows stood around her, crying and showing the robes and other clothing that Dorcas had made while she was still with them" (Acts 9:36–39). Similarly, Priscilla worked alongside her husband in their tentmaking business while also serving as a church leader and teacher. "There he met a Jew named Aquila. . . with his wife Priscilla. . . because they were tentmakers, as he was, he stayed and worked with them" (Acts 18:2–3). Our work has an impact on those around us.

These biblical examples offer crucial principles for today's working mothers. As Genesis reminds us, work itself was established by God before the fall: "The Lord God took the man and put him in the Garden of Eden to work it and take care of it" (Genesis 2:15). Whether we're in paid employment out of choice or necessity, our work can glorify God and serve His purposes: "May the favour of the Lord our God rest on us; establish the work of our hands for us" (Psalm 90:17).

These women's stories also help address the guilt that many working mothers feel. None of these biblical women are portrayed as 'having it all' in the modern sense, but rather as faithfully using their gifts and opportunities while trusting God with the results. "Each of you should use whatever gift you have received to serve others, as faithful stewards of God's grace in its various forms" (1 Peter 4:10). The biblical narrative shows us that we don't need to conform to any single model of womanhood to mothering style to please God, for "There are different kinds of gifts, but the same Spirit distributes them" (1 Corinthians 12:4).

Perhaps most importantly, these examples remind us to maintain an eternal perspective on our daily work. Whether we're leading teams, closing deals, or managing projects, our work has Kingdom significance. "And whatever you do, whether in word or deed, do it all in the name of the Lord Jesus, giving thanks to God the Father through him" (Colossians 3:17). Like Lydia's purple cloth business or Priscilla's tentmaking, our professional roles can become platforms for ministry, relationship building, and Kingdom influence. "Let your light shine before others, that they may see your good deeds and glorify your Father in heaven" (Matthew 5:16).

For today's working mothers, managing multiple roles can feel overwhelming. Yet Scripture reassures us: "Come to me, all you who are weary and burdened, and I will give you rest" (Matthew 11:28). The biblical examples show us that balance doesn't mean perfection, but rather faithful stewardship of the opportunities God provides. "She is clothed with strength and dignity; she can laugh at the days to come" (Proverbs 31:25).

These examples also teach us about priorities and wisdom in managing our various responsibilities. "But seek first his Kingdom and his righteousness, and all these things will be given to you as well" (Matthew 6:33). When facing difficult decisions about work and family life, we can take comfort in knowing that God promises to grant wisdom to those who ask: "If any of you lacks wisdom, you should ask God, who gives generously to all without finding fault, and it will be given to you" (James 1:5).

The testimony of these biblical women reminds us that we're part of a long line of women who have successfully integrated work, family, and faith. They demonstrate that our professional lives aren't separate from our spiritual lives but can be a vital part of our service to God and others. "For we are God's handiwork, created in Christ Jesus to do good works, which God prepared in advance for us to do" (Ephesians 2:10).

Most importantly, these stories assure us that God's grace is sufficient for the complex roles He calls us to fill. "But he said to me, 'My grace is sufficient for you, for my power is made perfect in weakness.' Therefore I will boast all the more gladly about my weaknesses, so that Christ's power may rest on me" (2 Corinthians 12:9). When we feel inadequate for the tasks before us, we can rest in the knowledge that "I can do all this through him who gives me strength" (Philippians 4:13).

Finally, let's be encouraged to view our work through the lens of worship and service. Whether in the marketplace, the home, or the community, our labour can be an offering to God. "Serve wholeheartedly, as if you were serving the Lord, not people" (Ephesians 6:7). This perspective transforms our daily work from mere obligation into an opportunity for ministry and witness, allowing us to "work with all your heart, as working for the Lord, not for human masters" (Colossians 3:23).

Ready, Set, Go

Many of you reading this will, like me, be in a secular job. Statistically, we may be the only Christian's that these colleagues are coming into contact with at this time, so we should be ready and prepared to shine the light of Christ. But are we?

Like I said earlier, I had barely given any thought into the theology of work, and how the workplace is where I can reflect the light of Jesus. I'd heard the odd sermon here and there, typically ending with the action points of praying for your colleagues and inviting them to church. Both good action points but our focus should be bigger—inviting them to the Kingdom rather than just our local church. A church visit is simply one step in that ministry.

We've looked at why work is important to a Christian. It's now time to think carefully about how we live that out. It's easy to brain dump it after closing this book but let's actually go and live for Christ seven days a week, not just on Sunday.

Here are ten biblical principles that really helped to get my mind and heart ready to do this. I've listed the Bible verses at the end of this chapter for you to pick one out each morning to read and pray over before you start work.

1. God cares about every detail of your work, the pointless meeting or boring email. He sees it and he actually cares about it, even when we don't (Colossians 1:16–17)

2. Work is worship. We reflect His image when we work (Genesis 1:27)

3. Our work, every job, always has an impact on someone and the wider community. It is deeply relational. We work to serve others and give generously (Acts 20:34–35)

4. Our work allows us to develop skills and rejoice in our God given abilities (James 1:17)

5. Our workplace is not an off switch to our Christian-ness. The Holy Spirit does not leave us as soon as we step foot in the office. We can trust that He is with us, giving us His gifts and fruits as he promises (Joshua 1:9)

6. Do we think God is as powerful in our office as He is on a Sunday at church? Surely God is in our workplace, loving our colleagues. He wants all people to be saved (1 Timothy 2:4)

7. Are we actively praying for the organisations we work for? God cares about that organisation, it would not exist without His sovereign will and He would love to hear our prayers for it (1 John 5:14–15)

8. Do the basic things really well. People notice. Excellence is infectious (1 Corinthians 10:31)

9. We can't do this work in our own strength. When we feel defeated about an upcoming task or project, remember you have God in you who absolutely can do it. Go the extra mile and trust the Lord will get us there (Isiah 40:31)

10. Work is always for His glory (1 Corinthians 10:31)

The Three and the Fruits

A week or so before my return, I decided to reframe my working days as "workplace ministry" days, viewing all activities and interactions as a way to love God and others. It used to be just an afterthought. This is, after all, the primary goal of my work. My job description is just the format in which I do it.

I like simple goals, so I've opted to commit to three people in my heart whom I will minister to. This includes the lady I job-share with, my manager and my manager's manager. Obviously, I will be aiming to reflect Christ to all those I interact with at work but these three people are the ones I am going to make a special effort to invest in. Setting this goal gave me clarity and took a lot of pressure off.

So, what does this look like? It involves taking time to listen and pay attention to their struggles, the things they love and their needs. Herein lies the entry points where I can meet them where they're at, serving them and praying specific prayers for them.

We are created to be relational. As we invest in our relationships with our colleagues over time, there will be natural opportunities to talk about Jesus. As you pray and wait for those opportunities, you can shine the light of Christ by living out the fruits of His spirit—love, joy, peace, patience, kindness, goodness, faithfulness, gentleness, self-control.

Love could look like sacrificing a long lunch break to help a colleague with an extra task. We can show joy by tackling our intense workloads without moaning. Peace is shown by trusting that our work is not our identity, but God is. Kindness could take the shape of a muffin left on a colleague's desk who is having a rough day. Goodness, the opposite of evil, is seeing the good attributes in our colleagues, so that our hearts are slow to anger when they inevitably annoy us. Faithfulness can look like making every effort to do the work we say you are going to do, writing a list so we don't forget. Gentleness may be calling out workplace bullying in a calm but firm manner. Self-control means not joining in with office gossiping. It may mean walking away or speaking up against it.

PAUSE: Take a moment to look at the fruits of the Spirit below, and jot down an example of what that might look like for you in your workplace.

Love	
Joy	
Peace	
Forbearance	
Kindness	
Goodness	
Faithfulness	
Gentleness	
Self-control	

"But the fruit of the Spirit is love, joy, peace, forbearance, kindness, goodness, faithfulness, gentleness and self-control. Against such things there is no law." (Galatians 5:22–23)

#OnlyGodCanJudgeMe

There are plenty of people out there who judge Christians and have misconceptions of them. But sometimes perhaps we believe the lie that they will all hate us and think and say horrible things about us if we were to share a shred of our faith. I would argue this is the devil at work. He would love nothing more than for us to be scared silent. But what if we assumed better of people? That they may respond neutrally or positively? In reality, this has actually been more common for me, than the anticipated hate and judgement I assumed I would receive. In the same breath, I need to be comfortable with being thought of as weird. It's not that bad. Besides, only God's judgement is the one that matters. That's why the Bible tells us, "The fear of man lays a snare, but whoever trusts in the Lord is safe" (Proverbs 29:25)

Jesus was seen as weird and a rebel in His day. He broke lots of cultural and religious norms, surprising the society around Him. Perhaps you can surprise your colleagues by breaking their misjudgements about Christians. That you're not this strange, boring, secretive cult member (I hope), but rather a person, like them, who loves baking, football, watching Netflix, a glass of wine and most importantly, Jesus. Jesus died so that we could be saved. God made us and loves us.

We share Jesus with them each day we choose to live like Him. When we act in love and kindness and goodness, they unavoidably get a glimpse of the Kingdom. It's inescapable as these are heavenly designs. There is also a need for them to verbally hear the gospel. But what good is that coming from the mouth of someone who seemingly lives unchanged? That's why our distinctive lifestyle and character as a Christian gives us credibility.

We also need discernment and wisdom. It would probably be unwise to storm into the workplace on your first day and declare at the top of your lungs that Jesus is returning (though factually correct). There is a time and a place to explicitly share the gospel in this way. The good news is that wisdom is a gift of the Spirit (1 Corinthians 12:6-11). As we invest in our relationships with colleagues and customers over time, we can continually pray for wisdom. Always assume and expect that the Spirit will answer, because He does. "The Spirit of the LORD will rest on him— the Spirit of wisdom and of understanding, the Spirit of counsel and of might, the Spirit of the knowledge and fear of the LORD" (Isaiah 11:2)

Bible Verses for Your Work Day

For in him all things were created: things in heaven and on earth, visible and invisible, whether thrones or powers or rulers or authorities; all things have been created through him and for him. He is before all things, and in him all things hold together. (Colossians 1:16-17)

So, God created man in his own image, in the image of God he created him; male and female he created them. (Genesis 1:27)

You yourselves know that these hands of mine have supplied my own needs and the needs of my companions. In everything I did, I showed you that by this kind of hard work we must help the weak, remembering the words the Lord Jesus himself said: 'It is more blessed to give than to receive. (Acts 20:34-35)

Every good and perfect gift is from above, coming down from the Father of the heavenly lights, who does not change like shifting shadows. (James 1:17)

Have I not commanded you? Be strong and courageous. Do not be frightened, and do not be dismayed, for the Lord your God is with you wherever you go. (Joshua 1:9)

But God demonstrates his own love for us in this: While we were still sinners, Christ died for us. (Romans 5:8)

And this is the confidence that we have toward him, that if we ask anything according to his will he hears us.

And if we know that he hears us in whatever we ask, we know that we have the requests that we have asked of him. (1 John 5:14–15)

But they who wait for the Lord shall renew their strength; they shall mount up with wings like eagles; they shall run and not be weary; they shall walk and not faint. (Isaiah 40:31)

There are different kinds of working, but in all of them and in everyone it is the same God at work. Now to each one the manifestation of the Spirit is given for the common good. To one there is given through the Spirit a message of wisdom, to another a message of knowledge by means of the same Spirit, to another faith by the same Spirit, to another gifts of healing by that one Spirit, to another miraculous powers, to another prophecy, to another distinguishing between spirits, to another speaking in different kinds of tongues, and to still another the interpretation of tongues. All these are the work of one and the same Spirit, and he distributes them to each one, just as he determines. (1 Corinthians 12:6–11)

"So, whether you eat or drink or whatever you do, do it all for the glory of God." (1 Corinthians 10:31)

Reflect and Act

Take five minutes now to think over the below reflective questions and pick one of the actions to take.

Reflective Questions:

1. How can I view my workplace as a ministry opportunity this week?

2. Which three colleagues can I intentionally invest in and pray for?

3. What unique gifts or skills has God given me that I can use to serve my team?

Practical Tips:

Make some scripture prayer cards

- Create small cards with the biblical principles from the chapter
- Keep them in your work bag or desk as daily reminders, or schedule them to pop up on your phone
- Use them for quick prayer and reflection during breaks

Have a morning preparation ritual

- Select one of the above workday Bible verses to meditate on before work
- Spend 5–10 minutes praying for your workplace and specific colleagues
- Ask God to give you wisdom, strength, and opportunities to serve

Book an accountability check-in

- Monthly coffee or video call with a trusted Christian friend
- Share workplace challenges and victories
- Pray together about your workplace ministry

Prayer

Father God,

Thank you that you created me and you created work. You create good things and you create all things for your glory. Help me to glorify you in all that I do. Holy Spirit, show me which colleagues I should specifically be investing in as I go back to work. Give me wisdom in how to talk about you with them. Please let your love overflow through me onto them. Thank you.

Amen

The Mum Stuff

IN PREPARATION FOR GOING back to work after 14 months off, I asked a few mum friends some of the many questions running through my head. There was so much to unpack, so I created an online survey which I sent round to my wider mum network.

When going through their responses, four main themes came up: faith, emotional/personal factors, practicalities and relational impact. I also asked them their advice and what they'd do differently, and now I get to share that with you! Let's dig in with the most important thing first—faith.

Faith

FOR MOST OF US, this transition of going back to work is hard. But it is a great opportunity to rethink our approach to work and go back with a sound theology of what it means to be a Christian in the workplace. We also bring with us to the workplace what God has taught us through early motherhood. Let's look at some fellow mama's reflections on this process.

Reflections from Mums

All for His glory

"I suppose I've always thought about the scripture "whatever you do, do it for the glory of God" (not sure if I've quoted exactly right!) I thought about this throughout maternity leave while changing nappies etc which often doesn't feel very glamorous at all, so it was encouraging to think that it was all for God's glory, and just as worthy as any other kind of work. I think going back to paid work my reflection would be the same, that I'm doing it for the glory of God, and not for myself or others."

More Than a Means To An End

"At the beginning, during my first pregnancy 5 years ago, I didn't necessarily think about this as much when I returned to work. I just felt as if work was a means to an end, a practical thing that was

necessary to meet household needs. Now more and more I'm seeing how faith and work are intertwined."

Work Without Reward

"I have a much bigger view and appreciation for the work of caring for children, and the labour that goes on inside the home. I see motherhood as being a lot more valuable and meaningful than I did prior to being on mat leave. I think this is because I realised just how hard it is, and because it took a different kind of resilience than what I had learned in my corporate roles. In paid employment, you get external rewards like pay and recognition, whereas the work of motherhood happens behind the scenes and for no pay, so you really have to find your inner motivation to keep going. For me, focusing on the fact that caring for children has a purpose for eternity helped motivate me and gave me a bigger view of the daily work at home. Also, children are constantly going through behavioural developments, which brings new challenges for us to support them through which requires immense patience and wisdom, which I have grown to appreciate and see as hugely valuable life skills."

Uniquely Gifted

"I had an unexpected redundancy from my job during my mat leave, meaning I needed to consider what would be next for my career when I returned. I thought about the fact that God gives us unique gifts, skills, talents and desires that we can use to bless others in our work. This led me to pursue my curiosity for coaching and the possibility of making this into a career, as it fulfilled my goal of flexibility in work hours, and my desire to use my skills and talents."

Meaningful Alignment

"Work for me has become more meaningful after having children. I can see how God's call for us to 'work as if we are working for the Lord' can apply to doing our best in the workplace. Going back after

children has allowed me to also choose what kind of projects to work on, to make sure they are meaningful and aligned to my Christian values."

A Godly Shift in Priorities

"Not my theology but I think my attitude has changed. I used to be very diligent and conscientious (still am!) but sometimes took that to the extreme where I'd be working above and beyond what I was contracted to and trying really hard. Now since my son came along my priorities have totally shifted. So, at work I'm still very hard working, but I'll happily drop anything at a moment's notice if my son is ill for example and needs to be picked up from nursery. He is now my priority. Previously I would have been very hard on myself for even needing to take a sick day when it was clearly needed. I would be anxious and come in to work at all costs. Now I have a more laid-back attitude, and I think of my son first and work second. I think that's also what God is calling me to—not that God wants me to give up work but just reframe my attitude to it and adjust my priorities. I'm called to be a Mum first, and Assistant Psychologist second."

Many mums find the process of going back to work hard. God, thankfully, sees that and gives us the strength we need to navigate this new chapter.

Reliance

"During my return to work after my second pregnancy 3 years ago, I felt God telling me that it was not by my strength alone. I relied on God heavily during this time."

Reassurance

"I think He was giving me a lot of reassurance that my son would be ok and that he would go with him. He started 3 days of nursery at the same time as I started back at work and so it was a really daunting

time. I wasn't able to focus very well at work for the first few weeks because I was so worried about my son. It's the first time we'd ever been apart like that in over a year! So, God gave me a lot of reassurance at that time that he would be ok."

Provision

"I think God was sharing that I needed to trust Him for financial provision. Making a career change and exploring self-employment meant that I wouldn't have the reliable pay check that I was used to from my corporate roles before, but I knew the reasons why I was pursuing the change, and I felt God's leading me to trust Him for provision."

So we've heard it from mums themselves—in this time God has shown He is reliable, He reassures and provides, He says we are uniquely gifted, He uses motherhood to shift our priorities, He shows us that work is not just a means to an end and that work, in whatever format it takes, is always used for His glory.

Reflect and Act

Reflective Questions:

1. How has motherhood reshaped my understanding of work and purpose?
2. Where do I need God's reassurance or provision as I return to work?
3. What unique gifts can I bring to my role that glorify God?

Practical Tips:

Write a Faith & Work Reflection Journal

- Weekly entry on how motherhood has changed work perspective
- Note moments of God's provision or guidance
- Reflect on workplace ministry opportunities

Create a Priority Alignment Worksheet

- List work and family priorities
- Identify areas needing boundary setting
- Pray over alignment with God's calling

Build a Workplace Support Network

- Identify 2–3 Christian working mums for support
- Monthly check-in about challenges and prayers
- Create mutual accountability system

Prayer

Heavenly Father,

Thank you that I am fearfully and wonderfully made. That every gift and skill you have given me is because you have made it so, and they can be used to love others and glorify you. So much has changed and is changing in my life, help me to trust that you do and will provide. Your Holy Spirit is with me always, nothing can separate us. Help me to have a healthy and loving attitude towards work, and glorify you in all my tasks and interactions. Give me strength when it feels like I can't do this.

Amen

Emotional and Personal

Before and After

HOW ARE YOU FEELING in the lead up to this life change? Pause here and set a timer for five minutes. Jot down all the thoughts and feelings you might be experiencing. As mums we don't always take a moment to check in on ourselves, so let's do that right now. Once you've done this, carry on reading to see what some other mums have said they were feeling about going back to work, and how things changed for them over time. +10 points if any match your list.

I am feeling/thinking. . ..

_____

_____

_____

_____

_____

_____

_____

_____

_____

_____

Before

"I was very nervous and worried that my son would find it hard to settle into nursery. I was also worried that colleagues would have changed in a year and I might not know so many people in my team when I went back."

After

"It definitely got easier over time. The turning point was after 4 weeks when my son finally stopped crying at the nursery drop off so I felt really reassured that he was having a good time and not sad and missing me."

Before

"I felt positive and supported in the lead up to returning to work because my husband and I had discussed what we felt comfortable with prior, and had a plan in place for childcare. I was navigating an unexpected career change so I was mostly thinking about all of the factors that came with starting a new business and learning a new skill."

After

"I've only been at this for 8 months, but I would say that establishing a pattern and routine has helped it become easier. I was pleasantly surprised with how quickly I was able to slip back into the working mindset and language of work etc. After a year out I thought this would be much harder, but it came back really quickly and was quite enjoyable too."

Before

"Denial. Dread. Cold feet. Wanting to resign but not able to financially (and I know in the long term I love my job and wouldn't really want to resign)"

After

"[It got] easier. I understood more of what was happening. Sharing my insecurities with my line manager helped."

I hope you can see the theme here—it gets easier. As I write this, I've been back at work for a grand total for 4 days and I can already feel things starting to ease. In fact, my mornings aren't as rushed as I was dreading and I just demolished 4 choccy biscuits and a hot cup of tea without having to hide them from my 1 year old—result!

As with anything, the balance of motherhood and paid work has its challenges. My son is distraught when I drop him off at nursery. On his first day, I could still hear him screaming from outside the building. I cried all the way home. I wasn't expecting to feel that emotional! It's good to mentally prepare for the hard stuff. Here's what other mums found challenging:

"Leaving my son at nursery for 3 days a week and seeing him cry a lot at the start!"

"Navigating the fact that our family provides childcare takes wisdom, and needs open communication and clear boundaries. There have been times that our parental preferences for things like screen time or behaviour have needed to be reiterated and this can cause some conflict, but it has been broadly fine. Parents can prepare for situations like this by being clear on what their boundaries and rules are as a team and then being confident in sharing those in a clear and loving way."

"My little one transitioned well to childcare for 2 days per week, and was with me the other 3 days—so managing his emotional transition was smooth. The biggest challenge has been starting something completely new and the uncertainty financially around running my own business."

"I felt very guilty for going back full time and like I should be trying part time to allow more time to spend with my son."

"Facts vs feelings. I might have felt that it was awkward returning to work, that I was not capable but this was just a case of a feeling trumping a fact which was that I still had a brain and I was just as capable as before!"

"New staff that had joined the team—difficult learning to get in with a new vibe in the office and private jokes."

"I don't have childcare so the most challenging thing was meeting young people [as a church worker] and looking after the baby. The baby had my undivided attention on maternity leave and she needed it! But suddenly I had to dig deep and take on much more responsibility but not let my care of her slide."

"New ways of working were expected of me but I was not trained in. Really dashed my confidence."

Don't worry, mum, it's not all doom and gloom. I know I've banged on about the hard stuff but that's only so things don't catch you off guard. Let's move on to some positive insights. This week, after dropping my son off at nursery on a crisp autumn morning, I went to my favourite local cafe and worked there for a few hours. I felt like such a corporate queen with my latte and laptop perched on the rustic table. Peaceful piano music playing in the background. I read my bible (for the first time in ages) before logging on. I walked home in the sunshine during lunch. I loved it. Here's what others enjoyed about going back to work:

"Allowing my little one to be in childcare (grandparents watch him) 2 days per week has given him a stronger relationship with his grandparents and the opportunity to do different activities than I would offer in our everyday routine. It's great to continue using my skills in a work context and leverage the unique ways that God has gifted me."

"I appreciate my work days SO much more than I did before and I love that I get to see undistracted task time as a privilege."

"*Rediscovering that I am equipped to do my job and remembering I am more than a mother. Also being able to sit and have a coffee in peace (when I did have occasion family childcare and could go to the office)*"

"*It was nice to get back to work and engage my brain in a different way in my job. I felt like I had grown a bit rusty in the year of mat leave.*"

"*Getting to work with clients again and carry out assessments etc. Basically just getting back into the day to day of the job and flexing those psychology muscles again!*"

"*Having a bit of a structure again—days were definitely very varied on mat leave.*"

"*Starting a coaching course and learning an entirely new skill and the adventure of all that goes with that.*"

"*Getting to re-develop relationships with other colleagues.*"

"*A salary at the end of the month!*"

Mother's Load and Mum Guilt

If you haven't heard of the term "mother's load" then you clearly haven't spent enough time on Instagram, and for that I salute you. Somehow the app knew I had recently given birth and it wasn't long before it made sure I knew all about the mother's load. And actually, it wasn't long before I started experiencing it for myself. The mother's load refers to all those invisible jobs, often mental, that fill a mum's daily life. This includes things like always thinking 10 steps ahead, medical appointments, managing the household shopping list, overseeing the families emotional needs, remembering birthdays and making sure the nappy bag stays stocked up. Our brains are always on, buzzing and juggling. And then eventually we have to throw managing our paid jobs into the mix too! Yippee! Oh, and let's not forget about mum guilt. The guilt of forgetting something, or feeling like you're not doing enough to meet your child's needs, comparing yourself to other mums and the guilt of leaving our little ones in childcare. I asked some of my mum friends how they're coping with this:

"*I'm not sure I've been brilliant at coping! But I'd definitely say just taking one day at a time and being kind to yourself—not layering on the Mum-guilt.*"

"*Having a supportive husband and accepting help from others is how I cope with the mental load. I communicate clearly when I need more help and my husband does SO much. We have clear designated tasks and I'm thankful that we've had six years of marriage to get to a point where we work well as a team. I have had moments where I found it hard to accept help from other people, but I have to remember that raising a child is not meant to be done alone. I'm also a big fan of having lots of family around as much as possible because it just feels natural that everyone is pitching in.*"

"*It is a minefield and there can be really hard days, combined with days that go really well!*"

"*[Mum guilt] made me feel like I was being a bad Mum for going back to work full time and abandoning my child.*"

"*I have felt this in the past, especially as a few of my family members are stay at home mums. What helps me is the helpful fact I work from home, a supportive husband, lots and lots of prayers and Proverbs 31.*"

Over the past year of motherhood, I've really felt just how much we need support from others to navigate the messy, beautiful world of being a mum. I've had to continually practice asking for help and accepting it when offered, to not fall into autopilot of just trying to do everything by myself. Recently, I've been feeling overwhelmed with the house chores and have worked to divide these up efficiently with my husband. This has really helped take the pressure off and learn to be served. In fact, I'd say he now probably does more than me around the house (life-giving). I'll unpack this in more detail in the "marriage" chapter and share a spreadsheet on how to divide up these tasks.

Identity Shifts: More Than "Just" a Working Mum

The journey of motherhood and professional life is a profound transformation that challenges our deepest understanding of self. Whether you're working full-time, part-time, or navigating a flexible arrangement, your identity as a Christian woman is rooted not in roles or work hours, but in your relationship with Christ. The transition from full-time motherhood to balancing work and family can feel like navigating uncharted emotional terrain. You are not "just" a working mum—you are a multifaceted, divinely designed woman with a complex and valuable purpose.

Society often presents a limiting narrative that suggests working mothers must choose between career and family, or that they are somehow compromising their maternal role by pursuing professional aspirations. This perspective fails to recognise the rich, nuanced reality of modern motherhood. Your identity is not defined by your work schedule, but by your heart's commitment to your family and your professional calling. Whether you're in the office full-time or balancing part-time hours, you model resilience, adaptability, and faithful stewardship to your children—showing them that passion, purpose, and parenting can beautifully coexist.

The internal dialogue of identity can be challenging across all working arrangements. You might find yourself experiencing moments of guilt, uncertainty, or feeling pulled in multiple directions. These emotions are valid and normal, regardless of whether you're working full-time, part-time, or in a flexible arrangement. Your worth is not measured by perfectly balanced spreadsheets or immaculately tidy homes, but by your heart's intentionality and your commitment to glorifying God in every sphere of influence. Embrace the season you're in, recognising that your current rhythm of work and motherhood is a unique expression of your calling.

Biblical women like the exemplar in Proverbs 31 demonstrate that productivity, entrepreneurship, and nurturing are not mutually exclusive. This passage portrays a woman who manages her household, contributes economically, supports her community, and is celebrated for her multifaceted capabilities. Whether you're working full-time or part-time, your professional journey is an opportunity to live out this holistic vision of womanhood—contributing meaningfully while maintaining your primary commitment to your family's spiritual and emotional wellbeing.

Finding Your Calling: Beyond Just a Job

Distinguishing between a mere job and a true calling is a spiritual journey of discernment and purpose. And to be honest, sometimes we can overthink it. Our calling is to keep God's commands—loving Him and others. We're able to do that in whatever setting, and I would argue God is more concerned with you keeping His commands than waiting for a specific job to do that in. As Christian mothers, we're invited to see our professional lives not as transactional exchanges of time for money, but as meaningful opportunities to steward our God-given talents. A job pays the bills; a calling transforms lives—including our own. This doesn't mean every role must be overtly ministerial, but that we can approach our work with intentionality, seeing it as a platform for growth, service, and Kingdom impact.

Discovering your unique calling requires honest reflection and spiritual attentiveness. It's about understanding the intersection of your passions, skills, and the needs around you. To learn more about your professional strengths, answer the following questions:

1. What work gives me the most energy, and what drains me?

2. What barriers are there that are stopping me from thriving at this job?

3. Where can I have the most impact on people?

God has specifically designed you with capabilities that extend beyond your current job description. Pray for wisdom to recognise how your professional skills can be channels of grace—whether that's through excellence in your work, compassionate interactions with colleagues, or using your professional platform to support meaningful causes.

The tension between practical necessity and spiritual purpose is real for working mothers. Your calling might look different in different seasons—sometimes it's a strategic career path, other times it's about maintaining skills while prioritising family. For me, it's currently the latter. What remains constant is the invitation to bring your whole self to your work: your creativity, integrity, and compassionate spirit. This is very hard when you've been up since 5am with a tantrum-prone toddler (every day this week for me). Your workplace becomes a mission field where your distinctive approach can demonstrate Christ's love through professionalism, kindness, and quiet faithfulness.

Biblical examples remind us that calling is rarely a linear or predictable journey. Take Esther, who found herself in a professional role she didn't choose yet used her position to bring about significant change. Or Priscilla, who worked alongside her husband in tentmaking while also being a pivotal support in early Christian ministry. Your professional path is not just about personal achievement, but about being available for God's unexpected assignments and Kingdom opportunities. While you might not always be aware of what He's doing through you, He is.

Dressing for Your Work Self

I feel like the past two years have been a mess when it comes to dressing for myself. My body changed in pregnancy, so things stopped fitting. My body changed all throughout recovery and mat leave, and again things didn't fit. Now I've got to find a way to dress for work when I've barely been able to dress myself for home! I love fashion and want to find a new style that works for my new body. But how much do I really invest when clothes still need to be accessible for breastfeeding and now that I'm pregnant again that's a whole new layer of challenge!

Okay, rant over. I've learned that comfortable, bloat friendly clothes that I can mix and match, layer up or down is going to be the most effective. A capsule wardrobe can help—3 tops and 3 bottoms, 2 jumpers/cardigans and 2 pairs of shoes that you can just mix and match for work. This way you don't have to add another task to your mental load of trying to figure out outfits in the morning. Us mums need to minimise that load where we can. Find items that are good quality, which will last and that you enjoy. One friend shares:

"I'm still trying to figure this one out! I can dress casually because I work remotely but I have attended some networking events in person and felt at a loss for what to wear. I think setting aside some budget to invest in clothing that fits and reflects the office style/job that you have is important because this has an impact on confidence. I feel like fashion has changed a lot since I went on mat leave and felt that my old professional clothes were becoming outdated, and I would love to have some timeless pieces for my work wardrobe."

Let me just say, she has a capsule wardrobe, and her outfits always look on-point #MumCrushMonday

Mums in Ministry

I appreciate that I am coming at the topic of returning to work from the perspective of working in a secular environment. I wanted to gain some insight from a mum who works for the church, so I interviewed Mia who works on the staff team for a church in the UK.

Navigating Ministry as a New Mum: Mia's Experience

When Mia (not her real name) returned to her role in church ministry after maternity leave, she quickly discovered that balancing the demands of ministry with the needs of her toddler brought both unique joys and significant challenges. Her journey reveals the beauty of integrating family life into ministry and the systemic gaps that churches often have when supporting mothers in leadership roles.

The Joys of Ministry with a Baby

"One of the unexpected positives of having my son with me in ministry is how he breaks the ice," Mia explained. "People can find it intense to sit across from me in a coffee shop and talk about their lives. But with the baby there, it's like the tension just melts away. He brings such a natural ease to our conversations."

Mia also shared how her son has become a beloved presence at church events. "He doesn't come to everything, but when he's at things like socials or barbecues, people love it. It's a great way to show them that ministry isn't just a job; it's part of my life."

The Invisible Load

Despite these positives, Mia is candid about the heavy toll of combining motherhood with ministry. Unlike her male counterparts, who often have spouses to manage the bulk of parenting, Mia feels constantly torn between roles.

"I've chosen not to put him in a nursery for now," Mia shared. "While that decision aligns with our family's values, it means I'm never really 'off.' I'm his primary carer during the day, so the only time I can concentrate on ministry tasks is in the evening after he's gone to bed."

She contrasted her experience with that of male pastors. "A male pastor can just focus on being a pastor because his wife tends to take on the parenting role. But on Sundays, I can't just be a church worker. I'm still Mum. I can't switch one role off to do the other. That's exhausting."

This lack of boundary has led to feelings of frustration. "It's not unique to ministry," she acknowledged. "In many workplaces, it's still the woman who's expected to drop everything when a child is ill or needs care. Mothers rarely have the same freedoms as fathers, even in so-called egalitarian households."

The Church's Role: Progress and Shortcomings

Mia's church had to draft a maternity policy from scratch when she became pregnant—a reflection of how rare it is for women in ministry to continue working after having children. "Throughout my pregnancy, I didn't know what I'd get in terms of pay," she recalled. "That uncertainty was incredibly stressful. I was constantly asking, 'Will it just be statutory? Will there be a gift? What do I plan for?' They eventually decided on six weeks at 90% pay and then statutory maternity pay. We couldn't afford for me to take much longer off, so I went back sooner than ideal."

The church's willingness to accommodate her desire to bring her son along to work has been a blessing, but Mia acknowledges that it's been a learning curve for everyone. "When I returned, there wasn't a clear plan for re-entry—no formal training or updates. I eased myself back in, which worked well for me, but for others, a structured re-entry might be helpful."

Balancing Church Ministry and Motherhood

Mia's approach to one-on-one meetings with people has had to adapt to her new reality. "I schedule meetings in the morning so my son can nap at home in the afternoon. We'll start with him in a highchair eating snacks—grapes and vegetables are my go-to—and then transition to a walk and prayer. Toys don't work; he's not interested. But eating and walking? That works for us."

Having her son present at meetings isn't without challenges, but Mia sees it as a creative solution that allows her to continue serving in ministry while being present for her child.

The Importance of Flexibility

The key to making it all work? Flexibility—both on Mia's part and from the church. "They've been understanding about my hours. If I need to shift things around or make up time later, they're fine with that. Ministry ebbs and flows. There are busy seasons, like

September, where I do more than my contracted hours. Then quieter times, like summer, where I can scale back."

She also credits her husband for stepping up in his own way. "Sundays are hard for him because our church has an afternoon service. He takes our son home on public transport while I stay for church events. It's a long, tiring day for both of us, but we're learning to share the load."

What Churches Can Do Better

Reflecting on her experience, Mia has some advice for churches looking to support mothers in ministry:

1. Establish clear policies: "Not knowing what maternity pay I'd receive was a huge source of stress. Churches need to prioritise this, understanding the emotional and financial impact of uncertainty."

2. Offer re-entry plans: "A clear plan for returning staff—training, updates on changes, and opportunities to ease back in—can make a big difference."

3. Be flexible: "Every mother's situation is different. Flexibility with hours and responsibilities is crucial."

Mia's journey highlights both the joys and complexities of being a mother in ministry. While her story is one of resilience and creativity, it also underscores the need for systemic changes in how churches support women navigating these dual roles.

Reflect and Act

Reflective Questions:

1. What emotions are you experiencing about returning to work after maternity leave? How do these align or differ from the experiences shared in this chapter?

2. What specific skills or passions do you bring to your workplace that reflect your unique calling?

3. How can you communicate and share the mental load with your partner or support system?

Practical Tools:

Mental Load Management Worksheet

Create a shared family spreadsheet with:

- Household chores
- Childcare responsibilities
- Emotional support tasks
- Personal self-care commitments

Then have a conversation with your spouse about how this makes you both feel, what can be delegated and what can be dropped.

Identity Reflection Exercise

- List 5 roles/aspects of your identity beyond "mother" and "worker"
- Identify how each role contributes to your sense of purpose
- Pray about integrating these roles holistically

Workplace Calling Exploration

- Skills audit: List professional skills
- Passion assessment: Note what energises you at work
- Kingdom impact brainstorm: How can you realistically serve others through your current role?

Work Capsule Wardrobe Planner

- 3 versatile tops

- 3 mix-and-match bottoms
- 2 layering pieces
- 2 comfortable shoes

Prioritise comfort, breastfeeding accessibility, and potential body changes

Prayer

Father, you created me and you love me. You are the builder of my identity. Help me to remember that my foundation is you. Please show me where I am holding on to guilt or trying to control too much. Give me and my spouse the skills to communicate lovingly and share the load and joy of parenting and working. Show me what I am not giving over to you. Give me space in the coming days to make small and meaningful changes for the good of my family and your glory. Amen.

Practical

ONE OF THE FIRST things on our to-do list in the lead up to going back to work is figuring out childcare. Nursery vs childminder? Grandparents? Juggling hours with spouse or mum friends? Where to even start?

The two things to first consider are what you are financially able to afford, and what your values are. For example, you may have a budget of £600 per month and would prefer your child to receive one-on-one care with a childminder (although they are often looking after 2–3 kids at any one time). As a part-time worker, my choice was limited by finances. We could afford 2 days of nursery per week, and that was only with the Governments 15 hours free funded hours. We're so fortunate to have my mother-in-law living just 20 minutes away and she, by the grace of God, agreed to have our son for one day a week.

Then it came down to choosing the nursery. I'll be honest, I just chose the one that was most convenient location wise. I could and should have probably explored more but it had good reviews and I was prioritising convenience. Convenience has been my currency of sanity. You might want to consider: funding options, location, carer-to-child ratio, development objectives, if food/supplies are included, accessibility, parking options and what their Ofsted report says. Here's what some fellow mums chose:

"Because we have my mum close-by, she agreed to help with childcare."

"My husband's parents had said from before he was born that they would be happy to provide childcare and we were happy to give this a try—so it wasn't a big decision, just happened naturally because of their desire to look after him."

"[Our decision was based on] proximity to our house. As we don't drive it needed to be easy to walk to so the decision was quite easy as there is a nursery two minutes from our front door!"

"I leave her with my parents once a month for a few days. I cried leaving her the first time but the second time I left the house with a spring in my step! My mum stayed home with me. I really didn't want to leave my baby in childcare. My parents were happy to help (they don't live close) so we had to be creative with how and decided a few days in a run once a month worked."

You can ask God to reveal to you what your priorities are, and ask local friends what they do and for any recommendations. Many nursery spaces get booked up a year in advance, so the sooner you start the process the more options you will have.

Let's Talk Money

Having a baby can be expensive, and putting our children in nursery/hiring childminders can add massively to this. I have been feeling quite stressed about finances lately. We completely depleted all our savings in maternity leave, I'm only part time so I'm not taking home as much as others, and now we're going to be paying just under £400 a month for 2 days of nursery. It has led to disagreements and cutbacks in our house. It has forced us to keep reminding ourselves that God has and will provide if something were to go wrong. I know I'm not the only one to worry about finances during this time. My friend has to be very strict with budgeting because her childcare costs over £1000 a month for just 3 days a week! The increasing cost of living and rising interest rates on mortgages are creating fear in our hearts. We need to strike a balance of wisdom in budgeting, generosity in giving and trusting in the God who would never leave us high and dry.

The NCT website helpfully breaks down the averages of the different childcare costs. To summarise, childminders tend to be slightly cheaper than nurseries, but it is important to consider what is included in the price (food, nappies, medicine etc).

Now is also a good time to sit down together and go through your savings, spendings and giving. Think about your financial goals as a family. I find thinking up to 2 years ahead helpful, as children's needs and life-stages are constantly changing. Speak to other parents or friends about how they are managing their finances and be accountable to one another.

Choosing Between Career and Motherhood

Becoming a mother can significantly shift our perspectives and values. You might find that you're either more or less career-driven than you originally thought. Many mums I've spoken to have even considered becoming full-time stay-at-home mums, only for an 'unmissable' career opportunity to arise. So, what do you do in that situation? How do you begin to navigate such a decision?

To help us explore this, I spoke to Vicine Koroma, mum of three and Head of Content at Squiggly Careers—a career coaching company that views career paths as 'squiggly' journeys rather than linear ones. Vicine also runs the Cultured Creator blog, where she reviews non-fiction books on career and personal development. She's the perfect person to help guide us through this decision-making process.

Vicine's Story

Vicine has always valued hard work, balancing studies and work from a young age. After starting her career in architecture, she realised the industry's long hours were incompatible with motherhood. When she became pregnant, she knew the traditional career path wouldn't support the changes ahead, and after her request for flexible work was denied, she began rethinking her career.

During maternity leave, Vicine explored freelancing, using her marketing skills to work with various companies. Inspired by feeling "stuck" in her previous job and a book called *The Squiggly Career*, she embraced flexible work that aligned with her family life. After connecting with the book's authors on social media, she landed a freelance opportunity with Squiggly Careers and decided to leave her architecture career.

By her second maternity leave, Vicine's side hustle had grown into a full business. Now, she balances work with Squiggly Careers, her own freelance marketing consulting and her Cultured Creator blog, redefining success by prioritising flexibility and fulfilment that supports her family and professional goals.

The Challenge of Decision-Making

Vicine tells us, "It's not just about you anymore. The decisions you make will impact your family, your health, and your sense of purpose. While the idea of career progression can be tempting, it's important to recognise that your choices should align with what you value most at this stage of your life."

She adds, "This is at the heart of 'Squiggly Careers.' Instead of viewing career moves as a ladder where you're always aiming to climb higher, squiggly careers encourage multiple pathways. Sometimes, this means making sideways or even temporary moves that are more in line with your current situation. Your career doesn't need to follow a linear path—it can evolve as dynamically as your life does."

Filters for Decision-Making

As a mum, the key to making informed career decisions is to use filters that help you determine what's truly important. For Vicine, those filters include **values** and **strengths**. Ask yourself:

1. What do I value most at this point in my life?

Is it family time, career advancement, financial stability, personal growth, or flexibility? Understanding your core values will help you make a decision that doesn't just make sense in the short term but aligns with your long-term happiness.

2. What role makes the best use of my strengths?

When considering a job, focus not only on what you're good at but also on what gives you energy. A role that drains you can impact both your professional life and your family life, whereas a job that aligns with your strengths will give you more energy, joy, and satisfaction.

3. What is the impact on my mental, physical, and spiritual health?

This is a crucial filter for mums. In the midst of career decisions, it's easy to overlook your well-being. If taking on a new role or climbing the corporate ladder means sacrificing your health or your relationship with your family, it might be worth reconsidering.

4. What is the opportunity cost?

What will you be sacrificing by making a career change or stepping up in your job? Will you lose precious time with your children? Will you feel stressed and overwhelmed? It's essential to think not only about what you'll gain but also about what you'll lose in the process.

Pause here and jot down your answers to some of these questions.

_____

_____

_____

_____

_____

_____

_____

_____

Balancing Aspiration and Reality

Vicine emphasises the importance of possibilities over plans. "Careers aren't always predictable," she tells us. "While you may have set plans in place, sometimes life presents unexpected opportunities. These options might not align with your original career vision, but they can lead to new paths that fit your family life better. Being open to these possibilities allows you to see how your work can evolve in unexpected and rewarding ways."

Practical Advice for Balancing Career and Family

Mums returning to work should remember that "balance" is often more of a season than a permanent state. Some seasons might require leaning more into work, while others might demand more time at home. Vicine suggests thinking about work as "service" rather than a means of personal gain. Work can be a way to serve your family, your community, and even yourself by fulfilling your personal calling. It doesn't always have to be about climbing the corporate ladder or achieving traditional success.

The idea of "squiggly careers" is a helpful lens here. Your career doesn't need to follow a straight line. You don't have to always strive for promotion or a higher-paying role. Sometimes, the best decision is to step sideways, take a slower pace, or even step back if it serves your family and personal well-being.

Reassessing Your "Success"

Vicine stresses the importance of reassessing what success truly means. "Societal expectations often place immense pressure on what 'success' should look like," she explains. "It's often defined by outward accomplishments like job title, salary, or status. But for many mums, true success might look entirely different. It could mean finding a work-life balance that allows you to spend time with your children or setting boundaries that protect your family's well-being."

She also encourages the idea of creating personal success statements. "Think about what success means to you," Vicine says. "Is it about making a positive impact on others? Achieving personal goals? Or is it about creating a fulfilling home life for your family? By defining success on your own terms, you create a framework that guides your career choices, particularly when societal pressures or comparisons try to push you in another direction."

The Role of God in Career Decisions

Vicine highlights the importance of keeping God at the centre of career decisions. "As Christians, it's vital to remember that God has a plan for each of us," she shares. "Our work, in whatever form it takes, is a calling to serve others. Even as we navigate the twists and turns of our career paths, God's character remains unchanging. He is with us through the highs and lows, guiding our steps as we seek His will in our work."

Reflecting on her own journey, Vicine recognises how God often presents unexpected opportunities. "Just as He led the Israelites along a non-linear path, He can lead us through the squiggly lines of our careers and motherhood," she says. "Trusting that God is guiding you brings peace when making tough decisions, knowing that He is faithful and will provide for you in every season."

Making career decisions as a mum requires deep reflection on your values, strengths, and goals. By embracing the flexibility of a squiggly career, you can make decisions that align with your family's needs and your personal aspirations. Most importantly, remember that God's plan for you is unique and special. Whether your decision takes you up the career ladder, sideways, or down a new path, trust that God is with you every step of the way.

Career Progression for Part-Timers

As Christian mothers returning to work after maternity leave, we often find ourselves wrestling with complex emotions and practical challenges. Career progression isn't just about climbing corporate ladders; it's about stewarding the gifts and talents God has entrusted to us whilst maintaining our primary calling as nurturers of our families. Your part-time journey can be a powerful testament to balanced, intentional living.

Understanding your professional value doesn't diminish your role as a mother—instead, it complements it. God equips us with unique skills and passions that extend beyond our home, and returning to work part-time can be a meaningful way to use those abilities. Your workplace becomes a mission field, where your integrity, work ethic, and gentle spirit can shine as a reflection of Christ's love. Remember that your worth is not defined by job titles or hours worked, but by your identity as a beloved child of God.

Strategic career progression as a part-time worker requires intentional planning and grace-filled boundaries. Communicate openly with your employer about your capabilities and aspirations. Many organisations are increasingly recognising the immense value of flexible, committed part-time professionals. Seek opportunities for professional development that align with your schedule—online courses, targeted training, and strategic networking can help you continue growing professionally without compromising your family commitments.

Practical steps matter, but so does your spiritual foundation. Regularly seek God's guidance through prayer, asking for wisdom in balancing work and family. Surround yourself with a supportive community of fellow working Christian mothers who can offer encouragement, practical advice, and prayer support. Your journey is unique, and comparison can be a thief of joy and purpose.

Facing Workplace Discrimination

Workplace discrimination against mothers is a painful reality that many professional women encounter. As Christian women, we're called to respond with both wisdom and dignity, recognising that our worth is not determined by workplace perceptions but by our identity in Christ. Bias can manifest in subtle ways: overlooked promotions, assumptions about commitment, or microaggressions that challenge your professional capabilities. These experiences can feel deeply personal and emotionally exhausting, but they do not define your professional value or potential.

Document any instances of potential discrimination, seek advice from HR or professional support networks, and approach conversations with professionalism and clarity. Your response can be a powerful testament to grace under pressure.

Your faith provides a profound source of strength and perspective during challenging workplace experiences. Biblical figures like Esther demonstrated how to navigate complex environments with integrity, wisdom, and courage. Your response to bias is an opportunity to model resilience, not through aggressive confrontation, but through consistent excellence, quiet confidence, and an unwavering commitment to your professional growth. Pray for discernment in each situation, asking God to guide your responses and protect your spirit.

Support is crucial in these challenging moments. Build a network of trusted colleagues, mentors, and fellow working mothers who can offer practical advice, emotional support, and professional guidance. Many organisations are increasingly recognising the value of diverse, inclusive workplaces. Seek out allies who can advocate for fair treatment and challenge systemic biases. Remember that your journey is not just about personal professional success, but about creating pathways for other working mothers who will follow in your footsteps.

Mum-trepreneurship with Tiny Humans

I am noticing a trend in new mums starting their own businesses within the first year or two of having a baby. After seeing how much us mums are capable of, it doesn't surprise me. Starting a business while mothering young children is less about perfect balance and more about creative chaos.

I interviewed Jana Berker, Career & Leadership coach at her company, Ascenda Coaching. She is married to Kenan, Mum to a toddler and one on the way. We talked through her experience of being made redundant on maternity leave and taking the leap to start her own business.

Personal Story and Career Change

Maryke: Could you share a bit about your journey—being made redundant on maternity leave, realising you wanted a career shift, and navigating that transition?

Jana: I was working at LinkedIn in talent acquisition—a dream job I absolutely loved. But I'd only been there for a couple of years, so when the redundancies came, I wasn't surprised. This redundancy coincided with my return from mat leave, and I started looking for other part-time roles because, after having a child, that was a non-negotiable for me. However, there were so few part-time roles available at my level of experience—10 years in HR. My choices seemed to be either taking an entry-level job, which I could have done right after university, or working full-time and then trying to negotiate part-time hours after proving myself during the probation period.

I did consider those options and even went through some interviews. But the more I reflected on my values, the more I realised the compromises were too significant. I didn't want to work more than three days a week. So, out of necessity, I started thinking about other possibilities. Coaching had always intrigued me, and this felt like the right time to explore it. It was a blend of necessity and curiosity that led me down this path.

Starting the Business

Maryke: Once you decided to start your own business, how did you get going? That first step often feels overwhelming.

Jana: Training was my first step—I did a coaching certification course. It provided structure and a clear path forward. The course lasted three months, and it was a real financial investment but one we had planned for. That's a key piece of advice: know your budget and what you're willing to invest because starting something new isn't free. Starting the business was also an exciting and energising time for me, I enjoyed the ownership of being my own boss and starting something new.

Overcoming Challenges and Fears

Maryke: What fears did you face during that period, and how did you handle them?

Jana: One of my biggest fears was that this might not be financially sustainable. But I realised I wouldn't know unless I gave it a go. Kenan, my husband, was incredibly supportive. We talked through everything—the finances, the time commitment, and the risks. We agreed on how much we'd invest and set a timeline of one to two years to give the business a fair chance. Having that plan in place and a supportive partner made all the difference. When I faced setbacks and thought about quitting to take up a job instead, he encouraged me to keep going.

We also talked a lot about our values around work and family. As Christians, we believe work is part of God's design. We both wanted to balance our careers with raising our son, Judah, and that foundation helped us stay aligned through the ups and downs.

Maryke: Was there any scripture or spiritual insights that guided you?

Jana: The image of planting seeds and patiently nurturing them really stood out to me. Business and parenting both require time and trust in God's process. I love seeing results, so it was a lesson in patience and faith. I had to remember that growth takes time, and this was a season of cultivating rather than harvesting.

Key Lessons Learned

Maryke: What lessons did you learn through this journey?

Jana: Trust the process and be consistent. Results aren't always immediate, and it's easy to get discouraged. Setting milestones and timelines helped me stay on track. There were moments of doubt, but small wins reminded me why I started.

Avoid comparison—it's so easy to look at others and feel bitter if they seem to be progressing faster. Focus on your own journey and the choices you've made. I had to remind myself of the reasons I chose this path and trust that God was in control of the outcome.

Advice for Other Mums

Maryke: What would you say to mums considering a career shift, starting a business, or returning to work?

Jana: Experiment! Take a small step forward and see what happens. You learn so much more by trying something than by over-analysing. You don't have to quit your job—test your idea in the evenings or at weekends. Most career changes aren't linear; they involve several steps and lessons along the way.

Maryke: For mums worried about being overlooked for promotions because they're part-time, what advice would you offer?

Jana: Show up and do your best work. If a company can't see your value because you work part-time, it might not be the right environment. Promotions might come slower, but that doesn't mean they won't come at all. Focus on what you can control—your work, your attitude—and trust God with the outcome.

Also, check your motives. Are you seeking promotion because it aligns with your goals and values, or because you feel you should? Sometimes, it's about accepting the trade-offs you've chosen. For me, the flexibility I have now is worth more than a higher salary.

Final Thoughts

Maryke: As a career coach, what do you want to say to mums navigating work after maternity leave?

Jana: Remember why you made the choices you did. Trust the process, stay consistent, and avoid comparison. Surround yourself with a support system that understands your journey. And above all, keep checking in with God—He knows the path ahead, even when you don't.

If you are starting a business, your business model must be flexible enough to accommodate unpredictable nap times, unexpected illnesses, and those magical moments when your toddler decides productivity is optional. Consider service-based or online businesses that offer maximum flexibility—consulting, digital products, or freelance work that can be managed during nap times or after bedtime.

Financial planning becomes crucial when juggling business launch and motherhood. Start lean and bootstrap wherever possible. Utilise free or low-cost digital tools, leverage your existing networks, and be strategic about initial investments. Your home can be your first office, reducing overheads. Consider micro-times for work: those 20-minute windows while your child plays independently, or late evening hours when the house is quiet. They add up without feeling overwhelming.

I personally use the times when I'm nap trapped in the car to work on my side-hustles!

Your faith can be a profound source of entrepreneurial strength. Treat your business as a calling to glorify God, not just an income stream. Pray for wisdom in decision-making, patience during challenging seasons, and discernment about scaling. Your unique perspective as a mother can actually be a significant business advantage—many successful businesses are born from solving problems you've personally experienced.

Practical boundaries are your lifeline. Communicate clearly with family about work times, create visual schedules for older toddlers, and be kind to yourself about productivity. Some weeks, business progress will be minimal. Other weeks, you'll achieve more than you thought possible. Embrace the season, knowing that your worth isn't measured by linear progress, but by faithful, intentional steps towards your goals.

Logistics

After deciding on childcare, we now enter the exciting world of logistics—the pick up and drop off. With that, comes the morning and evening routine. I found that the logistics was the thing I was most worried about. My husband is a shift worker and so I was left to manage about 90% of drop offs and pickups. I thrive on routine and efficiency so to ensure I had a smooth morning and evening, I got to planning. I negotiated to work from home, starting at 9 am. I knew it would be a 45 minute round trip for nursery drop off, including time for tantrums/hugs/comfort. I knew it would take 10 minutes to get shoes on, coats on and pram out of the garage. Breakfast is included at the nursery so thankfully I didn't need to factor that in, but my son is a huge grump when he wakes up so I planned for 20 minutes of cuddles and stories. I also set time for both of us getting dressed. I knew I'd not have time to also pack exercise into my day, so incorporated that into drop off. I put on my running gear and popped my son in the running buggy and off we went. Not only does this mean I'm getting some movement first thing, it also cuts down the journey time and I can leave the pram at nursery—big win! Then I'd be able to get home and shower and make myself a nice breakfast and hot cuppa. From waking up at 7 am, to logging on at 9 am, I've been able to do so much and by planning it out in chunks of time and it has never felt rushed. I always set an alarm 10 minutes before we're supposed to leave just to make sure time doesn't escape me.

PAUSE: Take a look at the table below. Write down how much time you need for each to figure out your timings.

To Do	Number of minutes needed	Time

Here's what other mums have said about how they navigate the morning and evening routines:

The Morning

"One of my prayers has always been around having a God-blessed morning routine. I think this is so important in order to set the day up for success for everyone in the family. It has taken a long time to get to where we are now, but a successful morning routine always looks like me (as mum) sacrificing my mornings so that I can wake up early, before everyone else, to do my morning devotional and set up little things like the boys lunch and check the agenda to make sure they each have what they need for the day. Like I said, it has taken a long time to get the routine right but children thrive on routine so getting it right is important for us. Little things that we separate responsibilities for between my husband and I (who makes

breakfast / who brushes teeth / who sets up the clothes the day before / who packs back) makes a big difference and helps mornings run more smoothly. We always try to pray as a family before setting off on our days."

"With my husband! When the boys were younger he would do all pickups and drop offs which allowed me to then work my hours."

"On my work days my husband drives our son to his parents home about 45 minutes away and works remotely from there once per week and then drives them back home in the evening. The other day of the week they travel to our home."

"My husband does the drop off as I leave too early for it. I do pick up if I'm home in time with traffic, otherwise he does pick up."

"One parent gets the child dressed and has some time at home for play or eating and then leaves the house while the other gets ready for work etc."

"For me there's no childcare in the morning because I leave at 6:45 am so my son is still asleep. My husband wakes him up at 8ish, brushes his teeth and dresses him then they walk to the nursery together."

"Getting her ready and giving breakfast early then handing over to my parents. My husband usually leaves for work earlier so can't help."

The Evening

"My mum and dad are a huge help. If they are looking after the boys they make sure they have eaten dinner and are bathed before we pick them up. On the days they aren't with my parents, we make sure to always eat together and have the boys in bed by 7 pm. This just means that I have to finish my work by 4:30/5 pm latest."

"I'm finished with work by my son's bedtime so usually both of us are home during his evening routine to do bath and bedtime routine as normal. If I have a late evening call for work then my husband does the bedtime routine and we plan for that."

"I normally get home at about 6pm, either me or my husband will have picked up our son. We chat and play a bit, then cook dinner, eat together as a family, wash up, put our son to bed with a bedtime story and prayer, sometimes a bath. Then normally my husband and I crash out on the sofa by 8.30pm!"

When Baby Gets Sick

It's no surprise that when our little ones go off to nursery/childcare they quickly pick up bugs and illnesses. My son managed to last 2 days before getting a cold. But what does this mean for our jobs?

In the UK, you're allowed time off to deal with an emergency involving a dependant. If your child falls ill you could take time off to go to the doctor and make care arrangements. Your employer may then ask you to take annual leave or parental leave if you want to look after your child for longer. There are no limits on how many times you can take time off for dependants. You do not have to do this in writing or give written proof. Your employer may want to talk to you if they think time off is affecting your work. Your employer may pay you for time off to look after dependants but they do not have to. Check your contract, company handbook or intranet site to see if there are rules about this. If you are not given time off for dependants, your employer may allow you 'compassionate leave'—this can be paid or unpaid leave for emergency situations. In the UK, your employer must not:

- treat you unfairly for taking time off, for example refusing you training or promotion
- dismiss you or choose you for redundancy because you asked for time off for a dependant
- refuse you reasonable time off

Here's what our fellow mums have done when their child has fallen ill:

"They go to my mum and dads and work for me and my husband goes on as normal. There have been a few occasions where one of us has had to take parental leave to cover for looking after the kids if they are too sick / contagious to go to my parents."

"This hasn't been an issue for us because of the fact that we have grandparents looking after him and he hasn't had any serious illnesses. If he has a fever we cancel any activities and make sure to give him more rest and take it easy at home."

"I took carers leave days off from work. I am entitled to 5 per year paid, 5 more at manager's discretion, and any after that are unpaid."

Weighing Up Work Environments: Home vs. Office

For some of us office workers, we have more say in how much we work from home versus the office. The decision between working from home and the office can be deeply personal, intertwining professional aspirations with family calling. Home-based work offers unprecedented flexibility, allowing mothers to seamlessly integrate professional responsibilities with family nurturing. You can be present for your children's key moments while maintaining career momentum. The ability to start a load of laundry between meetings or quickly prepare an evening meal represents a form of whole-life stewardship that aligns with biblical principles of intentional living.

However, office environments provide unique opportunities for professional and spiritual growth. Physical workplace interactions offer networking possibilities, mentorship connections, and opportunities to demonstrate Christ's love through daily interactions. The structured separation between work and home can provide mental clarity and professional development that home environments may not naturally facilitate. Colleagues become a mission field, where your integrity, work ethic, and gentle spirit can shine as a reflection of your faith.

Practical considerations significantly impact this decision. Home working requires robust self-discipline and intentional boundary-setting. Without careful management, work can bleed into family time, creating stress and reducing the quality of both professional output and family interactions. Office environments, conversely, demand more logistical planning around childcare and commuting. Each approach carries financial implications—from potential childcare costs to home office equipment investments.

Spiritual discernment is crucial in this decision. Pray for wisdom to understand which environment best allows you to fulfil your multiple callings—as a professional, a mother, and a follower of Christ. Some seasons may require different approaches, and flexibility is key. Your worth is not defined by your work location, but by your heart's commitment to glorifying God in every professional and personal interaction.

Commuting: Survival Tactics for Working Mums

The commute—we either love it or hate it. Yes, we might have managed to free ourselves from the morning's toddler tantrums, but now we're packed on a train with adults who look equally tantrummy. How can we make the commute work better for us?

Spiritual Pit Stops: Finding God in the Chaos

The commute can be your spiritual lifeline. Those precious moments between dropping off the kids and arriving at work is riddled with opportunity. Many mums thrive off structure and so structured prayer works best. You could use a prayer journal app where you can quickly jot down specific prayers for colleagues, family challenges, and personal struggles.

A morning commute routine could look like this:

- First 10 minutes: Worship playlist (I find my brain needs a warmup)

- Next 15 minutes: Structured prayer using ACTS method (Adoration, Confession, Thanksgiving, Supplication)
- Final 5 minutes: Listening and reflection

For me, I work from home. When I walk my son to nursery, I pop headphones in and either listen to worship music, a Christian podcast or catch up on any missed sermons. I confess I get distracted; I often rewind because I've zoned out thinking about my to-do list. I'm learning to not put too much pressure on myself to do it perfectly and make space for God's grace.

Biblical grounding is crucial. I'm reminded of Philippians 4:6— "Do not be anxious about anything, but in every situation, by prayer and petition, with thanksgiving, present your requests to God."

Me-Time Masterclass: Reclaiming Your Headspace

Noise-cancelling headphones are more than an accessory—they're a lifeline. I invested in (aka asked my Dad to buy) the Sony WH-1000XM4 headphones after realising how much mental space I was losing to commuter chaos. To this day I still kick myself for losing them on the bus.

Recommended commute activities:

- Meditation apps (Calm has excellent 10-minute guided sessions)
- Audiobooks. The Audible subscription is worth every penny for me, I hate books (she says as she writes one)
- Podcast learning

Podcasts I'm loving on Spotify:

- *Heaven in Your Home*—a podcast on God's heart on sex, marriage and His mission on the Earth
- *The Family Discipleship Podcast*—conversations on the important but ordinary work of leading at home
- *Bible Project*—all about the bible and theology

- *Faith in Kids Parenting in the Toddler Years*—a playlist for Christian parenting for kids under 5
- *Risen Motherhood*—how scripture applies to modern motherhood

Strategic Time Management: Maximising Efficiency with Purpose

Effective time management for working mothers is about intentional planning and grace-filled strategies. Meal preparation becomes a game-changer—batch cooking on weekends, using slow cookers, and creating flexible meal plans can dramatically reduce daily stress. Consider dedicating some time each weekend to preparing freezer-friendly meals that can be quickly reheated, transforming dinner time from a daily challenge to a smooth, purposeful routine.

Technology and smart systems are your allies in reclaiming precious time. Invest in tools that automate repetitive tasks: grocery delivery services, shared family calendar apps, and smart home devices can significantly reduce mental load. Create streamlined morning and evening routines with prepared outfits, packed bags, and pre-set breakfast options. Embrace the principle of working smarter, not harder—each efficiency gained is an opportunity to invest more meaningfully in your family and professional calling.

Delegation is a spiritual discipline, not a sign of weakness. At work, learn to prioritise tasks effectively, communicate clearly with colleagues, and set realistic boundaries. At home, involve family members in household responsibilities, turning chores into opportunities for teaching teamwork and responsibility. Your children can learn valuable life skills through age-appropriate tasks, and your partner can share domestic responsibilities. Remember, perfect homes and flawless work performance are myths—grace and intentionality are your true measures of success.

Spiritual disciplines can paradoxically create more time by providing clarity and peace. Morning prayer or scripture reflection, even if brief, can centre your day. Consider audio Bible plans or podcasts that can be listened to during commutes or household tasks. Batch your mental tasks, use productivity techniques like the Pomodoro method (working for 25 minute intervals followed by 10 minute breaks), and create margin in your schedule for unexpected moments of connection—both with your family and with God's guiding presence.

Preparation is Queen: Evening Strategy

Preparation isn't just helpful—it's survival. I can't give it enough credit. While I still have the energy, I like to set myself a timer and get through as much prep as I can the night before. Just knowing that I'm only going to dedicate 15 minutes to these tasks helps me not to dread them.

Preparation Checklist:

- Nursery bag: Spare clothes, comforter
- My work bag: Laptop, charger, notebook, emergency deodorant, snacks
- Lunch prep: Batch cook on Sundays, make leftovers when cooking dinner, portion into containers
- Outfit selection: Laid out with military precision, quick and easy thanks to the capsule wardrobe
- Slow cooker prep: Ingredients chopped, ready to switch on

Teamwork Makes the Dream Work: Shared Responsibility

Childcare isn't a solo mission. It's easy for us mums to try and do it all. My husband is a shift worker and I do end up doing more of the nursery runs. To prevent me getting overwhelmed and resentful, I look at our shared ICal for the month and when he's on a late shift I put his name down for drop off. This helps me to physically see that it's not just me doing it all, or fall into the trap of trying to do it all! In an ideal world he would do this himself, but I am a planner and this falls into my skill set and ways of thinking anyway.

Negotiation tips that work for manager and marriage:

- Be specific about what you need
- Show willingness to compromise
- Demonstrate how arrangement benefits both of you

Breastfeeding and Weaning

I'm aware not all of you reading would have been able to chose to breastfeed, so you may wish to skip this section. I found breastfeeding and returning to work to be a major worry. I always thought I would have stopped breastfeeding before going back to work and definitely before my son could walk. I absolutely hated the idea of a toddler running about and climbing all over me, pulling at my clothes for milk. But that's precisely what happened!

My son was a problem feeder and it took us 10 months for him to make significant progress with solids. I found this incredibly challenging. I compared myself to other mums and their babies, wondering what I was doing wrong. There were many tears on my part.

He had to start nursery when I went back to work and he found the separation anxiety really hard. By this point, I had reduced the daytime feeds, but he kept wanting three feeds in the evening and night, and asking for it during the day. The health visitor rightly advised me that stopping breastfeeding at this time would be too much change for him at once. I agreed, so I just had to ride out the clothes-pulling for another couple of months.

At the start, my breasts would become very swollen and uncomfortable while he was at nursery. I pumped while typing away on my laptop to avoid mastitis. However, the majority of mums I've spoken to didn't have to pump, likely because they weren't feeding as often as I was!

When we started to see signs that he was getting more comfortable at nursery and the whining for milk got worse, we decided to take action. We chose a period of shift patterns where my husband was home for four days and able to support me by distracting our son and telling him that "Mummy's milk is all gone". During this time, he actually fell ill with a cold, which I thought would make this ten times harder. In actual fact, because he had no appetite, it made it easier! He only asked for milk two to three times during that week, and after a few days, he had completely forgotten that "Mummy's milk" was a thing!

So, if you're still breastfeeding upon your return to work—that's absolutely okay! You don't have to stop, and you do what is right for you and your baby. Having a small pump that you can pop in your bra really helps, and you can get these second-hand for an affordable price. Don't spend a lot—you're not going to use it for long.

Generally, the advice is to wean off breast milk slowly, to give your body and your baby a chance to adjust. This looks like dropping one feed a day, gradually. But it took me far too long to learn that there is no right or wrong way to do this, so don't let it get you down.

Although, speaking of getting down, many mums report a drop in mood when they stop breastfeeding. This is likely due to hormones dipping. Oxytocin, the 'feel-good' hormone, rises when we breastfeed and drops when we stop. Prolactin, the 'calm' hormone, drops suddenly when breastfeeding also stops suddenly. It's helpful to be aware of this, so you and your partner can understand any mood shifts that might happen during this time.

Have a list of things ready to give you a boost, like your favourite snack or a lovely hot bath. Celebrate and praise God for your body and how it has sustained your child. I also had my husband take a picture of my last breastfeeding session and I love comparing it to the picture of my first one and seeing how my son has grown!

I recommend checking out the NHS guidance on stopping breastfeeding.

A Biblical Perspective on Weaning:
Celebrating God's Design

Weaning can be an emotionally challenging journey, but as Christian mums, we can approach this transition with profound gratitude. Our bodies are miraculous creations, designed by God to sustain and nurture life in the most remarkable way. From the first moments of pregnancy to the months of breastfeeding, our physical form has been a living testimony to God's incredible design of motherhood.

Even when weaning feels difficult—with hormonal changes, emotional ups and downs, and the bittersweet realisation that your baby is growing up—we can choose to praise God. We can thank Him for the extraordinary privilege of being able to feed and nurture our children, for the strength He provides through each challenging moment, and for the beautiful bond we've shared through breastfeeding.

Scriptures remind us that we are "fearfully and wonderfully made" (Psalm 139:14), and our bodies' ability to create, sustain, and gradually transition away from breastfeeding is a powerful reflection of God's intricate and loving design. As we move through this season, we can hold onto the truth that God is with us, supporting us through every stage of motherhood.

Day One, Week One, Month One

Getting through the first day, week and month are huge wins. Here's some ideas on how to navigate them.

First Day Back at Work

1. Start with Prayer

Begin your day by committing it to God. Pray for peace, strength, and focus, and ask Him to guide your interactions and decisions. A simple prayer like, "Lord, go before me today. Help me to work with integrity and grace and give me peace about leaving my child in Your hands," can set a positive tone.

2. Give Yourself Grace

It's normal to feel emotional or out of sync. If you feel over-whelmed, remind yourself that adjusting takes time and that God's grace is sufficient for you (2 Corinthians 12:9).

3. Pack Ahead to Reduce Stress

Prepare your work bag, lunch, and childcare essentials the night before. Having everything ready can ease the chaos of the morning.

4. Set Realistic Expectations

Don't try to conquer the world on day one. Ease into tasks and conversations, knowing that productivity will naturally build over time.

5. Stay Connected to Your Child

A quick check-in with your childcare provider or a photo of your little one can help you feel connected without distraction.

First Week Back at Work

1. Build a Routine with God

Incorporate time for prayer or Bible reading into your new sched-ule. Whether it's a quiet moment before your child wakes up or listening to a devotional during your commute, staying spiritually grounded will help you navigate this transition.

2. Communicate Your Needs

Be open with your manager and colleagues about your adjustment period. Let them know if you need flexibility while getting back into the groove.

3. Set Boundaries

It's tempting to overcommit to prove you're still a dedicated employee but remember that your family needs you too. Set realistic boundaries for work hours and commitments.

4. Find Comfort in Scripture

Reflect on verses like Philippians 4:13 ("I can do all this through Him who gives me strength") or Isaiah 41:10 ("Do not fear, for I am with you"). Write them down and keep them visible as reminders throughout your day.

5. Celebrate Small Wins

Did you complete a project? Make it through the day without tears? Celebrate those victories and thank God for His provision.

First Month Back at Work

1. Evaluate and Adjust

Take time to reflect on what's working and what's not. Are your morning routines smooth? Is childcare going well? Are there areas where you need more support or balance? Prayerfully consider adjustments and don't hesitate to ask for help.

2. Lean on Community

Connect with other Christian mums in your church or workplace. They can offer encouragement, practical tips, and prayer support.

3. Prioritise Self-Care

Your physical and emotional well-being matter. Make time for rest, exercise, and activities that renew your spirit, like a quiet walk or journaling.

4. Revisit Your Why

Reflect on why you chose to return to work. Whether it's for financial reasons, personal fulfilment, or long-term goals, grounding yourself in your purpose can help you stay motivated.

Balancing work and motherhood can feel overwhelming but remember that God is sovereign over every detail of your life. Trust that He will provide strength and wisdom for each day (Matthew 6:34).

Reflect and Act

Reflective Questions:

1. How am I balancing my roles as a mother, professional, and Christian?
2. What support networks do I need to develop?
3. What adjustments might I need to make to my current routines?

Practical Tools:

Create a Transition Prayer Journal

- Daily prayer request section
- Gratitude log
- Space to track answered prayers
- Reflections on work-life integration

Design a Weekly Planning Worksheet

- Childcare logistics
- Work commitments
- Self-care activities
- Family time prioritisation

- Spiritual practices

Write Your Personal Mission Statement Template

My Mission as a Working Christian Mother

Core Values:
1.
2.
3.

Professional Goals:

Family Priorities:

Spiritual Commitments:

Quarterly Review Date:

Prayer

Father God,

Thank you that nothing is outside of your control. You care so deeply about all the tiny details of my career and motherhood journey. Where can I go from your Spirit? Where can I flee from your presence? You are there in both. Give me wisdom in this decision, that whatever I may do I would yearn to do it for your glory.

Amen

Relational

OUR RETURN TO WORK can have an impact on our relationships with our spouse, child, colleagues and friends, in good ways and bad. We're now going to explore that and hear from how other mums have experienced their connections change.

Marriage

Marriage is an ever-evolving relationship, which is part of its beauty. It likely changed when you got pregnant, and then when you had your baby and now it's about to go through the motions of you going back to work. Let's hear from some mums on how this transition impacted their marriages.

"It has meant we are both a lot more tired so have to be very intentional about making quality time to spend with each other. [My husband] has taken on a lot more of the domestic tasks like cooking and cleaning. It is an even split now whereas while I was on maternity leave I did a lot more of it"

"It has pushed us to rely even more on one another as a team. It's important to have open communication about work and how much time each person will spend with work activities. I think the key here is to support one another and just keep an open dialogue about what's working and not working and adjust as needed. For example, I realised I wasn't getting enough work done in 2 days per week, so we added a half day on a Saturday. This required my

husband to do more solo, but it also meant we balanced it so that it worked for all of us. We've talked about the importance of time as a couple and have protected one night a week as a date night (although we stay at home most times). We have worked hard to view the time we invest in our marriage as time we invest in our family because marriage is the foundation. We say yes to offers to watch our son so we can go out and do fun activities because this helps strengthen our friendship and joy which makes us better parents."

"[My husband has given me] lots of emotional and practical support! I think at times he has felt pressure to provide more income for the family to take pressure off me, but we've been able to communicate about this in a way that keeps a healthy mindset and balance of trusting God to provide for our future."

"My husband has been so supportive with both of my returns to work. He took on a lesser role in our second pregnancy just so that he could help more around the house and with pick-ups and drop offs. He has since been promoted but this sacrifice really helped at that time."

"I think it was hard for my husband to lower expectations of what I could do in the home now I wasn't a stay-at-home-mum. Also, it was hard for him to adapt to being more responsible for our daughter on a weekend when I have to work. But it is also nice learning to work together with him taking leave and getting time alone with her."

Are you seeing what I'm seeing? There seems to be two themes of a) husbands having to step up and do more around the house, and b) to both be intentional in carving out quality time together. I can also see how one feeds into the other! When the household is being looked after together, it can make it easier to look after each other.

Now is a really good time to reflect on how tasks are divided up in your household. Now that my little one is on the move, I can't just plop him down while I tidy the kitchen or do the laundry. I felt burnt out. To my husband's joy I created a master spreadsheet that accounted for all the physical and mental work that it takes to sustain this family. We sat down and took ownership of the specific items that worked within our strengths. Just the idea of trusting that my husband is going to lead on his tasks, from start to finish with no input from me, freed up so much headspace. There's lots of online quizzes you can do together about running the household to identify any imbalances. You can check out the spreadsheet I made by scanning the QR code below. I know that not everyone reading this will have a supportive spouse, or a spouse at all. It's so important we ask our church family for help. It's how God intends us to relate to one another, and people love to feel helpful. I'm not a single mum, and so I'm not in a position to offer wisdom on navigating motherhood solo. But here are some things I have heard that may helpful:

- Develop strong church and friendship networks. This shouldn't be all on you. The church should be looking out for you. If they're not, speak to a staff member to encourage them to think about how the church can be better at this. If you're not a single mum but reading this section, please do this too!

- Create intentional support systems. Who can you go to for practical support, and who can give you emotional support?

- Consider mentorship programmes in the church/Christian community

- Even when it feels like you're doing this all by yourself, remember God's promise of never leaving you alone

Marriage Reflection

Like a health check, it's important to pause and review if things are working properly. I recommend working through these questions together a few weeks before you go back to work and then 3 months after:

1. How have our relationship dynamics changed?
2. Where are we struggling to communicate?
3. What practical steps can we take to support each other?
4. How can we prioritise our relationship amid busy seasons?
5. Where do we need to extend grace to each other?

Our fellow mums shared the importance of quality time during this transition and thereafter. Here are some specific strategies for connection. I want you to pause right now and pick one that you're going to do this month:

- Monthly relationship check-ins
- Shared hobby or learning experience
- Individual and couples counselling
- Church community support groups
- Technology-free quality time

Biblical marriage isn't about perfect performance, but about grace-filled partnership. Ephesians 5:21 guides us: "Submit to one another out of reverence for Christ"—a radical invitation to mutual support and understanding.

Above all, don't forget to pray together. It's a powerful weapon against the enemy and a marriage rooted in prayer is a strong one. Try consistently praying for:

- Wisdom in managing family and work
- Patience during challenging transitions
- Continued love and understanding

- God's guidance in your partnership
- Strength to support each other's dreams

Friendships

After the rhythm of friendship has likely changed since having a baby, it's now going to take another shift upon returning to work. I could no longer meet up with mum friends or shift-working friends in the middle of the week for a coffee. I now have to plan ahead to meet them before church on a weekend. This means asking my husband to solo-parent for a few hours. It eats into the time we spend together as a family. It is therefore important to recognise that there is a cost to maintaining friendships. It's a good cost, but it requires constant checking in with your spouse. Are you both getting enough time with friends, whether that's with the kids or without? Is one of you struggling while the other person spends too much time with other people? Here are some questions to ask each other:

Friendship and Time Management Questions:

1. How are we balancing individual friendships with our family time?

2. Do you feel comfortable with the amount of time I spend with friends?

3. Are we both getting enough social connection outside of our family unit?

Practical Logistics Questions:

1. How can we support each other's need for friendship and social connection?

2. When I want to meet friends, what would make you feel most supported in solo-parenting?

3. Are there ways we can trade off "friend time" so we both get breaks?

Emotional Check-In Questions:

1. Are you feeling resentful about any time I spend with friends?

2. Do you feel like our friendship connections are sustainable with our current lifestyle?

3. How can we communicate more openly about social needs and constraints?

Spiritual Partnership Questions:

1. How can we pray together about maintaining healthy friendships?

2. Are our individual friendships contributing positively to our marriage and family?

3. What boundaries do we want to set to protect our family time while supporting individual connections?

It's fairly common to have to book in to see a friend two months in advance. There is a culture of busyness and a fear of an empty calendar. I was speaking to a fellow mum recently who was going through a hard time and desperately needed the support of her best friend, but her friend didn't have any availability for another 6 weeks. How sad it is when we trap ourselves in busyness that we fail to be available to be present for those who need us. I am guilty of this, too. So, what can we do about it?

Direct Communication

Have an honest, non-confrontational chat and express your feelings without accusation. Ask if everything is okay in their life, don't make assumptions.

Realistic Expectations

Accept that people's capacities differ and recognise current life pressures (work, parenting, personal challenges). A hard one but don't take it personally, unless they've told you otherwise.

Spiritual Perspective

Pray for understanding and patience and seek God's wisdom in navigating the relationship. Remember grace works both ways, but if they don't give you grace you still get to give grace to them.

Friendship Maintenance Strategies

Offer low-pressure connection methods like sending quick texts or voice notes. I'm awful at texting so I live for a voice note. I also tend to do "photo dump" updates to friends as a picture speaks 1000 words, right?

Potential Red Flags:

- Consistent one-sidedness
- Zero reciprocal effort
- Repeated cancellations without alternative suggestions
- These are signs it could be time to hit 'pause' or even 'stop' on that friendship. If it's draining you and taking you away from God and your family then it doesn't need to continue. It's up to you whether you let it fizzle or have a firm but kind conversation, not in anger, with the person. Perhaps seek advice from a wise third-party.

On a more positive note, I have found many friendships to have deepened during this time. While frequency may be reduced, the quality of the time I spend with certain friends is great. The spiritual dimension of friendship becomes more apparent in these seasons. True friendship reveals itself not through constant presence, but through consistent love, understanding, and grace. Friends who can hold space for each other's current life realities—without judgment or expectation—demonstrate a Christ-like approach to relationships.

The Bible offers profound insights into the dynamic nature of relationships. At its core, friendship is a divine design where love transcends convenient moments. Proverbs 17:17 beautifully captures this essence, stating that "a friend loves at all times, and a brother is born for a time of adversity". This suggests that true friendship isn't about constant availability, but about heart connection and unwavering support.

Just as life moves through seasons, so do our relationships. Ecclesiastes 3:1 reminds us that "to everything there is a season", a wisdom that applies deeply to friendships. Not every season requires the same intensity of interaction, and that's perfectly acceptable. Our connections ebb and flow, shaped by life's complex rhythms of work, family, personal growth, and spiritual journey.

Jesus Himself modelled a nuanced approach to relationships. He maintained an inner circle with Peter, James, and John, while also nurturing broader networks of disciples and connections. Each relationship had its own depth and frequency, demonstrating that varying levels of friendship are not just normal, but intentional. Christ's relational approach teaches us that spiritual maturity in friendship means understanding individual capacity and offering grace.

Mature friendships recognise that life changes impact connection. They understand that love persists beyond constant contact, and that grace covers the gaps in communication. It's about the heart posture—a commitment to care, even when practical engagement might be limited. The biblical model invites us to respect personal limitations while maintaining a spirit of compassion and understanding.

Ultimately, biblical friendship is a reflection of God's own character—patient, understanding, and unconditional. It's not about perfect performance or rigid schedules, but about love that endures, adapts, and remains steadfast through life's changing seasons.

Connecting with your child

Entering childcare marks a profound emotional journey for many mothers. The initial separation can feel like a seismic shift in your connection with your baby. Where once you were the primary source of comfort and interaction, now your child is developing relationships and experiencing the world beyond your immediate presence.

Emotional landscapes will undoubtedly change. You might experience a complex mix of guilt, anxiety, and unexpected grief. Some mothers feel a sense of loss, worrying that their bond might weaken. However, research and experience demonstrate that this transition can actually strengthen your relationship when approached with intentionality and grace.

Quality becomes more important than quantity. The moments you spend together—morning cuddles, evening routines, weekend interactions—become more precious and concentrated. You'll likely find yourself more present and attentive during these times, compensating for the hours spent apart.

Communication with childcare providers becomes crucial. Detailed handover conversations, requesting photos, and understanding your baby's day helps you feel connected. Many centres now use digital platforms allowing parents glimpses into their child's activities, which can be wonderfully reassuring. I adore seeing what activities my son has been up to in the day.

Motherhood is a profound spiritual journey, and childcare transitions reveal deep theological truths about trust, surrender, and God's encompassing love. When you release your child into a new environment, you're practicing a beautiful metaphor of faith—trusting something precious to another's care while knowing God remains constant.

Scripture offers powerful perspectives on this journey. Just as Hannah dedicated Samuel to temple service, modern mothers can see childcare as a form of dedication. You're not abandoning your child, but creating opportunities for growth under divine supervision. Proverbs 22:6 encourages training a child in God's way, which extends beyond your personal presence. When I dropped my son off at nursery for the first time, he screamed his head off so loud I could hear him down the street. I cried all the way home. But I kept reminding myself he is safe, and this is good for our family. I was instantly struck how easily I fail to see that when I feel like God is being quiet and leaving me in suffering. But He knows I'm safe and works all things out for my good, just as I try to do for my son.

Prayer becomes a transformative tool during this transition. Each morning, you can spiritually cover your child, asking for protection and blessing. You're partnering with God in your child's developmental journey, not just managing a logistical challenge.

This season invites deep spiritual reflection on attachment. Your connection with your child mirrors God's relationship with us—constant, unconditional, and not dependent on physical proximity. Your love remains unchanged, just as God's love remains steady regardless of our circumstances or location.

Practically, this might look like:

- Developing morning and evening prayer rituals
- Creating short prayer moments during drop-off and pick-up
- Journaling spiritual insights about your child's growth
- Seeing childcare as a collaborative journey with God

Your spiritual maturity during this transition can profoundly impact your child's understanding of faith, trust, and divine love.

Here's some helpful insights from other mums:

"He's become a lot more confident around other babies/children."

"I've been pleasantly surprised with my son's adaptability and affection for his grandparents. Perhaps I would've seen these traits regardless, but it's been something that I've noticed and is an encouragement."

"My eldest took a little longer to settle at nursery but we were very intentional about the type of nursery he went to (small / family vibe) so settling in didn't take too long."

"I value my days and my time with him so much and I'm thankful that we still have our special bond and that I know everything that is happening with his development."

"I always try to connect with him on pick-up and have a conversation or just some time to nod. Together after pick-up. This has helped the reconnection after the separation of work and nursery"

"Excitement in both of us to see each other after a day apart."

I can really relate to that last one. I genuinely get butterflies in the moments before picking my son up. He always runs to me and gives me the biggest hug, just like the father welcoming home the prodigal son in Luke 15.

Family

Our relationships with family can also be affected as you go back to work, particularly for those who are relying on grandparents for childcare. We knew we wouldn't be able to afford three days of nursery per week and would benefit from having Granny take my son on a Tuesday. But I was nervous about asking her. It's hard work and I felt bad placing that on her. He is ultimately my child and my responsibility, why should I put that on someone else? I had to do a lot of thinking about how to have that conversation. I encouraged her to take her time and think about it. Thankfully she said yes and we came up with a plan together. She is one of the most kind and gracious people I know, and I am forever thankful for how she supports our family. I made sure to check in with her after a month to see how she's finding it and if there's anything we can do to make it easier. My son adores his days with Granny, and their routine of playgroup in the morning and park in the afternoon.

Here's a guide of how you can go about asking family for regular childcare:

1. **Preparation:**

- Write down your specific needs (days, hours, duties)
- Consider what support you can offer (groceries, fuel money, meals)
- Think through potential concerns they might have
- Have alternative suggestions ready if they need to decline

2. **Setting Up the Talk:**

- Choose a calm, private moment
- Make it a dedicated conversation, not a rushed aside
- Consider starting with "I'd like to discuss something important about [child's] care"

3. **During the Conversation:**

- Start by acknowledging their existing support and relationship with your child
- Be direct but gentle: "We've been looking at childcare options, and I wanted to discuss something with you"
- Present the situation honestly, including your financial constraints
- Be specific about what you're asking: "Would you be open to having [child] every Tuesday?"
- Express that you understand it's a big ask
- Give them space to voice concerns or hesitations
- Be clear that it's okay to say no

4. **Important Points to Express:**

- "We value your relationship with [child]"
- "We understand if this isn't something you can commit to"
- "We want this to work for everyone involved"
- "We can discuss ways to make this manageable for you"

5. **Practical Considerations to Discuss:**

- Backup plans for when they're unwell or need time off
- Clear expectations about routines and rules
- Emergency contact information
- Any financial support or compensation you can offer
- Whether it's a trial period or ongoing arrangement

Follow-up:

- Give them time to think it over
- Offer to discuss further or answer questions
- Be prepared to accept a "no" gracefully
- If they agree, plan regular check-ins to ensure the arrangement is working

Signs the Conversation is Going Well:

- They ask detailed questions about the arrangement
- They share their own ideas or suggestions
- They express enthusiasm about spending more time with their grandchild
- They start problem-solving with you

Things to Watch For:

- Hesitation or discomfort in their response
- Immediate concerns about their physical capabilities
- Mentions of other commitments or time constraints
- Non-verbal cues suggesting reluctance

Remember, this conversation might need to happen over multiple discussions. It's okay to start with "I'd like to explore this idea with you" rather than asking for an immediate commitment.

Scripture consistently emphasises the importance of family relationships and mutual support across generations. The command to "honour your father and mother" (Exodus 20:12) extends beyond childhood into adult relationships. The book of Ruth provides a beautiful example of intergenerational care and family loyalty. Proverbs 17:6 states that "grandchildren are the crown of the aged," suggesting the special joy and purpose grandparents can find in their relationships with grandchildren. The early church model shown in Acts and Paul's letters demonstrates how believers cared for one another as family, sharing resources and responsibilities. Timothy's own faith was shaped by his grandmother Lois (2 Timothy 1:5), highlighting the spiritual impact grandparents can have. The biblical concept of family extends beyond mere biological ties to encompass mutual care, support, and nurturing relationships that reflect God's design for community.

Childcare Providers

Establishing clear expectations begins before you even sign the childcare contract. Let them know your family's specific needs, values, and non-negotiables. This isn't about micromanaging but creating mutual understanding. Include practical details like your child's routine, dietary requirements, comfort objects, and any specific behavioural or developmental considerations. Think of it as a relationship blueprint that provides both structure and flexibility. We gave our nursery a picture of us to put up near my son's coat peg so he could see mummy and daddy anytime.

When something becomes challenging, approach the conversation with a collaborative mindset. Start with positive affirmation—acknowledge the provider's hard work and good intentions before diving into concerns. Use "I" statements that focus on observation rather than accusation. For instance, "I've noticed my child seems anxious after certain activities" is more constructive than "You're doing something wrong." Come prepared with specific examples and, if possible, potential solutions or alternatives you'd like to explore together.

With childminders, create a communication framework that feels comfortable for the both of you. Agree on preferred communication methods—whether that's daily brief chats, a communication book, or a dedicated messaging app. Schedule regular formal check-ins, perhaps quarterly, to discuss your child's development, address any emerging concerns, and realign expectations. These meetings are opportunities for honest, graceful dialogue that prioritises your child's well-being.

Cultural and personal differences can sometimes create communication challenges. Approach these moments with genuine curiosity and respect. If something feels misaligned with your family's values or your child's needs, seek to understand first. Ask open-ended questions that invite dialogue: "Can you help me understand how you typically handle this situation"? This approach demonstrates respect for the provider's professional expertise while creating space for collaborative problem-solving.

And let's not forget to pray for those looking after our little ones. This is a profound act of spiritual warfare and love that transcends the practical boundaries of your relationship. These individuals spend significant hours nurturing your children, shaping their early experiences and interactions. Your prayers can be a powerful covering, asking God to fill their hearts with patience, kindness, and genuine care that goes beyond professional obligation.

Consider specific areas of prayer that align with the fruits of the Spirit. Pray for love—that those caring for your child would have a genuine, compassionate heart that sees beyond tasks to the individual child's emotional needs. Pray for joy, that they would find delight in their work and in the children they care for. Ask for peace to guide their interactions, especially during challenging moments. Pray for patience—a supernatural ability to respond with grace when children are testing boundaries or experiencing emotional turbulence.

Oh, and a card and choccie bar on their birthday always helps!

Time for Another Baby?

Our son is 17 months old now, and we're starting to entertain the idea of having another baby (actually, two weeks after writing this I just found out I'm pregnant again, so this is timely!). It's exciting to imagine a little sibling for him, but I won't lie—I feel scared and unsure. It's not just the thought of sleepless nights and endless nappies all over again (although that's part of it); it's also the fact that I've only been back at work for two months.

The transition back to work was a big leap. I had just begun to feel like I'd regained a piece of myself—my professional identity—and now I'm thinking about pressing pause again. The idea fills me with a mix of emotions: guilt for not wanting to "stay on track" with work, fear of how another pregnancy might affect our family dynamic, and even a little sadness at the thought of dividing my attention between two little humans.

But then, there's the other side: the joy of giving my son a lifelong companion, the thought of a full, bustling house, and the deep-down knowing that children are a gift from God (Psalm 127:3). Did you know the sibling relationship is likely the longest relationship we'll have in our lifetime? It's a tug-of-war between my head and my heart.

To make a decision this big, I've learned that it helps to break it down into smaller, practical steps.

1. Assessing Work and Family Balance

Returning to work after maternity leave taught me how important it is to have systems of support. If we were to have another baby, I know I'd need to evaluate how my workplace could accommodate another pregnancy and subsequent leave. Are there policies or benefits that could ease the transition?

It's also worth thinking about childcare arrangements—what would we need to adjust if we were managing a toddler and a newborn? These are big questions, but they're easier to face when written down and tackled one by one.

2. Checking in on Our Marriage

Having a baby is a team effort, and adding a second one will only increase the load. My husband and I have had a lot of honest conversations about how this might impact us as a couple. Would we need to reassess how we share responsibilities? How can we keep our connection strong during the chaos?

3. Being Realistic About Timing

There's never a perfect time to have a baby, but there might be better or worse times depending on our circumstances. Would it make sense to wait another six months to feel more settled in my role at work? Or would waiting feel like putting life on hold unnecessarily?

As Christians, we don't make decisions in isolation. I've been leaning into Scripture and prayer, asking God to guide my heart and mind as I navigate this uncertainty. Proverbs 3:5–6 reminds me to "Trust in the Lord with all your heart and lean not on your own understanding; in all your ways submit to him, and he will make your paths straight."

When I feel overwhelmed by the "what ifs," I need to pray: "Lord, I don't know the future, but I trust that You do. Help me to lean on Your wisdom and not my fears. If this is Your will, give me peace and prepare me for what's ahead."

I've also found comfort in talking to other mums in my church and community. Many have faced similar crossroads, and hearing their stories has reminded me that I'm not alone. God often uses others to provide the encouragement and clarity we need.

Ultimately, I know that God's timing is perfect. My prayer is that we'll follow His lead, trusting that He will equip us for whatever lies ahead. This decision isn't just about logistics—it's about faith and surrender, letting go of the need to control every detail and trusting that He will meet us there, no matter what.

Reflect and Act

Reflective Questions:

1. Where do I need to extend grace to myself during this transition?

2. How can I intentionally nurture my marriage during this busy season?

3. How can I maintain meaningful friendships while balancing work and family?

Practical Tools:

Marriage Connection

Implement a weekly 30-minute "State of the Union" chat where you:

- Review household task division
- Discuss upcoming schedules
- Share appreciation and emotional check-in
- Pray together about your relationship and family

Child Connection

Create daily reconnection rituals:

- Morning blessing/cuddle before drop-off
- Dedicated 15-minute undistracted play time after work
- Bedtime storytelling with specific focus on their day's experiences
- Use conversation prompts like "Tell me about something that made you smile today"

Friendship Maintenance

Develop low-pressure friendship strategies:

- Send weekly voice notes instead of lengthy texts
- Schedule quarterly catch-ups with key friends
- Use shared digital platforms (photo sharing, quick messaging)
- Be transparent about current capacity and energy levels

Prayer

Heavenly Father,

Thank you that you designed us to be relational. Help me to know how to love those around me well, especially as things are changing again. Help me to be kind and graceful like Jesus. Give me strength to set healthy boundaries. Above all, help me to lean on you through the power of your Holy Spirit.

Amen

Final Reflections

Navigating Motherhood
and Work with Grace

As you journey through this season of balancing work and motherhood, remember that your worth is not defined by your productivity, perfect parenting, or professional achievements. Your identity is rooted in God's love and purpose for you.

Soak yourself in scripture. God provides the strength you need when challenges feel overwhelming. Your Christian values and understanding of your deeper "why" will be an anchor during difficult moments. Be intentional about seeking God's guidance through prayer, Bible reading, and counsel from trusted, godly friends.

Be compassionate with yourself. You are doing an incredible job navigating multiple complex roles. When guilt or stress creep in, pause and list the things you're proud of. Celebrate your resilience, your love for your family, and your commitment to both your professional and maternal calling.

Expect a season of adjustment. The first few months will involve teething problems—renegotiating household tasks, managing new childcare arrangements, and finding your rhythm. Give yourself grace and time. Avoid making significant decisions during this initial transition period. Communicate openly with your partner about feelings, challenges, and needs.

Talk transparently with your workplace. A supportive manager can help create flexibility and understanding. Consider a phased return or flexible working arrangements that support your family's unique needs.

Remember, this journey is not about perfection but about faithful, loving presence—for your children, your partner, your workplace, and most importantly, in your relationship with God. Trust His guidance, remain flexible, and know that you are more than capable of navigating this season with grace and strength.

As we come to the end of this book, I've asked fellow mums for their final reflections and advice to help guide you on your way.

"Soak yourself in scripture. God gives you strength. Know your Christian values and your why, it will help you on the harder days."

"Be kind to yourself and remind yourself of your why, and list the things you're proud of if you start to feel guilt or stress."

"The topic of motherhood and work is loaded with societal expectations, economic pressure, opinions formed from our upbringing, and our faith. There are a lot of factors to consider, not to mention the opinions of friends, family members, and perhaps even strangers. This is a topic with a lot of pressure. It's important to seek the Lord through prayer and Bible reading, and to gain input from Godly people as we reach our own conclusions about what is best for our family. I'd encourage mums to keep an open mind and maintain flexibility in their mindset and actions to adapt to the needs and stages of balancing work and family life. I really enjoyed the book: The Mission of Motherhood by Sally Clarkson, and the podcast by Ruth Chou Simmons called GraceLaced."

"Talk about how you feel with your partner. Then, after a few weeks, talk about how you feel with her manager. They can reassure / make things clearer or easier (if a good manager!)"

"Be kind to yourself—you're doing an amazing job!!"

"Don't expect it to work well for the first few months—there are teething problems e.g. who does what now you're not at home, juggling pickups and different types of childcare. Give it a few months before making any big decisions (like changing working hours). It gets better."

When I asked these mums if there was anything they would have done differently, they said:

"I would have reduced my hours sooner."

"Perhaps put less pressure on myself. Felt a sense of needing to achieve everything all at once, but could just trust the Lord more in the process of starting up a business."

"Perhaps I would have done a phased return and built up to full time more slowly."

"I'm a planner—so I would have tried to get myself out of my phase of denial that I was returning so I could plan in advance. I was left scrambling to make it work once I returned and that was stressful."

Closing Prayer

Heavenly Father,

I come before You in this season of transition, feeling the weight of motherhood and work. Thank You for the gift of children, the blessing of meaningful work, and Your unending grace.

Lord, strengthen me when I feel weak. Guide me when the path seems unclear. Remind me that my worth is not in my productivity, but in Your unconditional love. Help me to trust Your plan, even when I cannot see the full picture.

Bless me with wisdom, patience, and resilience. Provide supernatural energy when exhaustion creeps in. Cover my children with Your protection. Support my marriage and friendships during this challenging season.

Give me courage to be gentle with myself, to seek help when needed, and to remember that You are faithful in every moment. Help me to see my work—both at home and professionally—as a calling and a ministry.

I trust You with my family, my career, and my heart.
In Jesus' name, Amen.

www.ingramcontent.com/pod-product-compliance
Lightning Source LLC
Chambersburg PA
CBHW052151090426
42741CB00010B/2219